CONTINGENCY
SEAMANSHIP

CONTINGENCY SEAMANSHIP

Coping with the Unexpected in Harbor and at Sea

John Clemens

ZIFF-DAVIS BOOKS/ *New York*

Contents

Introduction

It's late Sunday afternoon.

You're finishing a perfect weekend cruise, just eight miles from the harbor. A 20-knot breeze off the port beam propels you toward home. The Tahitian sunset is spectacular, suggesting a continuation of fine weather. One of your guests passes a glass of wine up to you.

Everyone aboard is enjoying in his own private way that paradise that comes only to sailors. The hypnotic sounds of your 30-foot sloop gliding through the water blend perfectly with the strains of the Beethoven symphony wafting out of the stereo speakers below.

For perhaps the first time in your life, you think you understand what the word *tranquility* really means.

Your reverie is interrupted, however, when you notice a distinct change in the color of the water off the starboard bow. Incredulous, you stand in the cockpit for a better view. Your heart begins to race as you realize that you are much too close to a rocky shoal you'd intended to clear by a mile.

Just three seconds after you throw the rudder over hard left, the bow crashes into a jagged wall of rock lurking below the surface. Two of your friends lounging below are thrown out of their seats by the force of the impact. The noise of the collision is awesome, reminding you of a grand piano falling from a great height.

Your boat is dead in the water, heeling 30 degrees to starboard, the sails luffing wildly. One of your female guests is screaming, her hysterical shrieks interrupted only by the the awful grating of the hull as the boat bashes again and again into the rocks.

You are horrified as you look below and see a half foot of water above the cabin sole.

One of your guests, life jacket in hand, climbs into the cockpit, looks pleadingly at you, and says, "What do we do?"

A sailor's horror story?

Sure.

Fiction?

Absolutely not.

The rock we hit was just two miles off the French Mediterranean coast, near St. Tropez.

I have not always been so unfortunate. Most of my cruising experiences have been far less complicated. Almost always we've managed to be snugged down in port before the really bad weather arrived. I have never once entered one port thinking it was another. It's been ninety-nine percent pleasant.

But, I have collected my fair share of personal horror stories, ones I'll never forget. And I've listened to many others told me by sailors I've met along the way.

One common thread seems to weave its way through most of these sailors' tales: lack of mental preparation.

In most of the cases, the skipper involved became confused and disoriented because the problem he faced was entirely new to him. After all, you don't run aground with great frequency. And you may sail all your days without facing a *real* man overboard emergency.

There is a false sense of security that lulls the sailor into feeling that crises just don't happen to him, or—worse—if they do, he'll figure something out. "After all," he thinks, "I've read all the books. I've been sailing for a long time. I'm ready for whatever comes!"

There's a lesson here. It is that very little of the sailor's experience or study prepares him adequately for the uncommon emergency. In the midst of chaos at sea, the mentally unprepared mind has a nasty way of short-circuiting very quickly.

Think about your last boating misadventure. I've watched enough scenes between skipper and crew from the comfort of my cockpit to know that, whether it is your new boat hook floating away under the next pontoon or a genuine, certified emergency, the normally rational human being has an inexplicable capacity to retrogress to lower animal behavior in times of severe (and not so severe) stress.

How, then, can a sailor become mentally prepared?

I believe that something must be added to experience and book learning. It is *simulation.*

Simulation is a way to consciously imitate problems a cruising sailor might face. It is a technique that brings the problem alive. Instead of remaining in the pages of a textbook, the reader becomes part of the problem and the primary source of the solution. It's what training experts call "skill training." And it's as much a part of the required drill for a cruising skipper as it is for the pilot of a jumbo-jet.

Contingency Seamanship is a collection of simulated problems that sailors typically must face while cruising. Because each of the problems is simulated, the reader has the opportunity to experiment and try out various solutions without running the risks of placing his boat and crew in distress.

You won't be reading detailed sections on piloting, anchoring, sail-tuning, or any of the scores of topics discussed so well in hundreds of other sailing books.

The simulations in *Contingency Seamanship* represent problems the cruising sailor might encounter any time. Some are so nonthreatening as to seem almost humorous. Others are real crises which can jeopardize your boat and crew if you are unprepared. They can become all-too-real horror stories if you don't know what to do.

Each situation is fully developed so that you have the information to assume the role of skipper. As skipper, it will be up to you to decide what to do to prevent a minor problem from erupting into a catastrophe.

There is one thing I've learned while doing the research on *Contingency Seamanship.* There usually are no simple, pat answers for the kinds of problems that can occur while cruising.

Consequently, I've avoided, wherever possible, formula solutions. You won't see checklist answers like "the ten steps to proper anchoring." Certainly, such checklists have their place. Too often, however, their inflexibility just doesn't jibe with the real world.

Each simulation does have its "book" solution, however. They're provided so that you can learn by comparing what *you would do* with the approach others would take. These "book solutions" are composites gleaned from discussions with scores of sailors I've met, plus three years of researching every book on sailing I could find.

The purpose of *Contingency Seamanship* is to help you simulate typical problems so that when the real crisis occurs, you'll be ready. Odds are better than 100 to 1 that you won't have time to search through your on-board library for a solution. Even if you did have the luxury of time, there's something particularly ominous about a skipper hurriedly paging through *Chapman's* while his boat drags toward a lee shore in a gale.

I believe that you can be far better prepared as a skipper if you "re-file" much of your boating knowledge *by situation.* Organize it by realistic, natural categories instead of chapters and subsections typical to most books. Prepare it for quick retrieval.

Many sailors suffer from "data overload" when an emergency occurs. They're so inundated with information that they don't have a clear picture of what to do. This is not surprising. Much of their knowledge has never been brought together into useful categories.

The technique of learning by simulation used in *Contingency Seamanship* helps to solve this problem. There are three steps. *First,* read through one of the simulated scenarios. Be sure you understand the problem fully. *Second,* using the blank page following each situation, write down the actions you, as skipper, would take to solve the problem. It's important that you spend a good bit of time on this write-up, using as much of your knowledge and experience as possible. And, be sure that you don't refer to the book solution until you've finished writing down your own approach to the problem.

Third, read the "book solution" for the situation you are working on. Compare what you would do with the *Contingency Seamanship* recommended solution. Remember that the book solution is a composite, constructed from discussions with other experienced sailors and reviews of what has been written on the subject. It's very possible that you may not agree totally with the book solution. That's fine. There are no absolute answers to these problems.

The important thing is that you spend some time *thinking* about the problem. Simulating the solution. Associating solution steps with the problem.

I believe that when you and your crew have completed study of the simulated cruising problems in *Contingency Seamanship,* you will be better mentally prepared for the unexpected—those minor and major crises which are as much a part of sailing as wind and water.

Preparing yourself for sailing means more than getting the boat ready, more than anti-fouling, varnishing, and engine-tuning. *Really* being prepared means accomplishing mind-training, too.

That's the whole idea behind *Contingency Seamanship.*

CONTINGENCY SEAMANSHIP

SITUATION 1:
Dragging Anchor

You've anchored for the night in a small, protected bay with a light breeze off the land. It's a perfect spot, you think, and with a scope of 8:1 on your nylon rode, you and your crew are comfortably asleep.

At two A.M., you are awakened by the noise of increasing wind and the uncomfortable roll of the boat. Going up on deck in your pajamas, your suspicions are confirmed. The wind has shifted almost 180 degrees and is blowing a Force 5. The anchor is dragging.

There are breakers to leeward, about 300 meters off. You have no reserve anchor.

You decide not to leave until daybreak due to unmarked rocks in the entrance.

You figure you've got about 20 minutes before your boat wrecks on the beach.

1

HERE'S WHAT I'D DO . . .

Any boats downwind? Or rocks close by? If not, take some time to attempt to reset the anchor. This can be done by paying out several fathoms of anchor rode and giving an occasional sharp pull to get a new bite. Take a few turns around the bitt and snub the line from time to time.

If the anchor does not hold, start the engine and go forward just enough to take the strain off the line, then let the anchor reset. Once you get up to a scope of 10:1 or so, and she still drags, it's time for more drastic action.

You can increase the holding power of your anchor by using a sentinel. This is a weight (a piece of pig iron or ballast is perfect) sent down the anchor rode with a suitable line to stop it a little more than halfway to the anchor.

This may sound easy now. But remember, it's dark and your boat is pitching. You'll want to have a line which is marked for length already attached to the sentinel. And the sentinel will need an easy attachment system for hooking it onto the rode. If you use chain, the sentinel will need to be attached with a roller to facilitate easy paying out.

Once the sentinel is down, it should improve the situation in at least two ways. First, it will cushion the pull on the anchor as the boat surges in the swell. Second, it will decrease the angle of pull on the anchor, increasing its ability to dig into the bottom.

If the sentinel fails to do the trick, and you are still dragging toward the beach, get under way using motor or sails and locate a more protected spot.

One of the best ways to prevent dragging is to be sure the anchor is properly set in the first place. There is only one way to do this with certainty: an underwater inspection. Assuming you snugged down in your anchorage with some daylight remaining, this inspection can be part of your before-dinner swim.

SITUATION 2:
Loss of Engine

Your favorite restaurant across the bay is on a canal bank just downstream from large industrial locks. You've tied up starboard-side-to with a nest of four boats.

When you and your party return from dinner and are preparing to get under way, one of the "helpful" and slightly inebriated crew members in the next boat casts off your stern line before you give the order.

You immediately order your bow line cast off, start your engine and back, handily fouling the stern line in the screw.

Your engine will not start and you have no steering control, as the stern line was pulled taut around the rudder.

It is dark, and you are drifting with the strong canal current toward the breakwater's jagged rocks. You have only minutes to act.

4

HERE'S WHAT I'D DO . . .

SITUATION 2 *Recommended Solution*

You probably have only one option in this case: drop the anchor and drop it fast!

If you are one of those sailors who stow their anchor below under the canned soup, scuba gear, and miscellaneous ropes and lines, you may find yourself redesigning your main cabin by brute force, while darting topside repeatedly to see just how near you are to the breakwater.

Always have an anchor ready on deck for this kind of emergency.

Your friends in the boat which was to starboard may get under way and offer you a tow to safety, and you will no doubt accept it. But don't expect that first line tossed to connect with your panicky bow crew. Get the anchor down first, and *then* attempt the tow. Remember, too, that being towed without steering control is enormously difficult.

SITUATION 3:
Loss of Rudder

You and your guests have been caught out in a Force 8 in your 24-foot cruising auxiliary. While you were hove-to waiting for the weather to moderate, sternway damaged the rudder pintles. Consequently, you've lost your rudder.

Wind and seas have now calmed enough for you to attempt a run to the harbor, 30 miles away. When you check for fumes, prior to starting the gasoline engine, you discover that the fuel tank has ruptured, emptying about ten gallons of gas into the bilges.

As you pump out and ventilate, you try to decide what to do. You have no radio aboard and no other emergency distress equipment.

HERE'S WHAT I'D DO . . .

SITUATION 3 *Recommended Solution*

Although you've lost the rudder and the engine is inoperable, you can still make it to the harbor without too much trouble.

After getting the sails up, you'll find you can steer the boat by varying the amount of weight placed fore and aft. Have several of your crew move up to the bow. This will cause the forward part of the boat to dig in a bit more deeply, turning the boat into the wind. Move weight aft to turn downwind.

Sail trim can also be used to steer. With just the jib up, the boat will tend to turn downwind as the center of effort moves forward. The opposite effect, a tendency to turn upwind, will result from sailing with just the main up.

With both sails up, a bit of fine-tuning will balance your boat, enabling her to sail in a fairly straight line relative to the wind. For example, luffing the main while flattening the jib will tend to turn the boat downwind (the center of effort moves forward). Conversely, luffing the jib while flattening the main will cause the boat to round up into the wind. Thus, you can tack by letting the jib run free while hardening up on the main.

Steering by sail alone to windward or on a reach presents no great problems. But, if you must run before the wind, the chance of an accidental jibe is too great. Use just the headsail poled out.

Finally, a drag can be fashioned out of a spare sail or sea anchor. Attach it to the stern, rigging it so you can move it from side to side, causing the boat to turn. Also, it may be possible to rig an emergency rudder using your spinnaker pole, whisker pole, or dinghy oar. Lash a board to one end and counterweight the other with internal ballast or an anchor. Attach this makeshift helm and rudder system to the stern pulpit.

SITUATION 4:
Running Aground

You've spent a beautiful morning in a new cove you've just discovered. Leaving shortly after noon on a rising tide, you run aground on sand while pointing out the sights to your guests.

Your sloop is tilted jauntily over to starboard. She bumps heavily on the sand bottom as the slight swell lifts and drops her. Your crew members are getting a bit panicky, and you're quickly losing your temper.

What do you do?

HERE'S WHAT I'D DO . . .

SITUATION 4 *Recommended Solution*

The first thing to do is get the sails down as quickly as possible. If you were running before the wind, they'll drive the keel further onto the bottom.

Check to be sure that the boat is not taking any water. If she is, you'll want to attempt repairs before moving the boat into deeper water. Likely she is still sound, and this grounding will be like most: a minor, but embarrassing, inconvenience. Here's what to do.

Review what's happening with the tide. You left the cove on a rising tide. You're lucky, since as time passes, the rising water may lift your boat off the sand.

Resist the overwhelming temptation to start the engine immediately and reverse with full power. Chances are much too good that you will simply suck more sand under the keel. Instead, get a kedge anchor out quickly. Use your dinghy to row out one of your anchors. Attach the line to a stern bitt and let it pay out as you row.

If you do not have a dinghy readily available, you can swim the anchor out, floating it on a life preserver. One additional approach, although a long shot at best, is to throw the kedge out and then snug it.

Once set, keep the kedge line as taut as possible. Now is the time to start the engine, but put it into forward instead of reverse. The propeller will wash some of the sand from beneath the keel. Remember to apply as much pull to the kedge line as possible.

Have one of your heavier crew members swing out on the boom. This massive leverage will increase the heeling angle and may loosen the keel. Or, have the entire crew "sally ship" by moving together from port to starboard and back repeatedly. This should get you loose.

15

SITUATION 5:
Fouled Anchor

The sun hangs low in the western sky. Your guests are lazily, somewhat unhappily, stirring, realizing that a truly perfect day is just about over.

Your anchorage, in a little-known cove 12 miles from the marina, was a perfect choice.

You start up your engine and station a crew member on the bow to take in the rode as you carefully position the bow over the anchor. As if to prove the bitter comes with the sweet, the anchor refuses to break out.

Unable to resist the desire to prove your superior strength, you put the engine in neutral and go forward. After coming very close to giving yourself a massive hernia, you return, perspiring heavily, to the cockpit.

Your anchor is still fouled. Wondering why it didn't work as well on your last cruise when you dragged in a Force 7, you decide what to do.

HERE'S WHAT I'D DO . . .

SITUATION 5 Recommended Solution

First, after snubbing the rode tightly to a bitt, try running slowly over the anchor for a few meters. If this doesn't clear it, pay out a few more fathoms of line and run slowly around the anchor in a circle, keeping the line taut. You may foul the rode on one of the exposed flukes, but so much the better! This could "trip" the anchor out.

If you're still stuck, motor around to a position 180 degrees from where you anchored, avoiding fouling your propeller by having one of your crew constantly tend the anchor rode. Now exert backing pull. This pressure, opposite to the way the anchor "set," should get it out.

Still stuck?

Position the bow directly over the anchor and snub the rode down as tight as possible. As the boat pitches in the swell, it will exert massive pull on the anchor, possibly freeing it.

If the anchor still does not break free, you may decide to don diving gear and investigate the problem at the source, being extra careful not to become fouled yourself. At this point, you should consider abandoning the anchor temporarily. Attach a float (one of your fenders or an empty bleach bottle will do fine) to the anchor line so you can locate the anchor when you return.

One of the best ways to prevent fouled anchors is to use an anchor trip line. This line, attached to the shank of the anchor and held at the surface by a small buoy, is an almost foolproof anchor retrieval system. It lifts the anchor out "backwards." Also, it indicates to other boats where your anchor lies, discouraging another skipper from laying his anchor line over yours.

SITUATION 6:
Using Spring Lines

You've spent the night comfortably berthed alongside the leeward side of a dock. About ten the next morning, the wind veers and strengthens considerably. Your pleasant berth becomes increasingly uncomfortable as the seas head through the entrance of the small harbor. Your boat crashes against the dock as it's lifted by the growing swell. You decide to get under way quickly and locate a safer and more comfortable spot.

You have little maneuvering space dockside, however, because a 60-foot motor cruiser is just four feet ahead of your bow and a houseboat is tied up just ten feet aft of your stern. Both are untended.

By the time you're ready to get under way, the wind and seas are so strong that your crew finds it impossible to push your bow away from the dock. You feel you can't clear the motor cruiser safely.

What's the best way out of your berth?

HERE'S WHAT I'D DO . . .

SITUATION 6 Recommended Solution

There is always the possibility that you could safely get under way using boat hooks, muscle and an heroic burst of engine power. Probably too risky, though.

A far simpler way, and much more seamanlike, is to rig an after bow spring line. Here's how.

Before you cast off the other lines, secure a line to the bow cleat and run it to a dock bollard at about the midships position. After you've cast off the other lines, station a crew at the bow with a large fender.

Now go ahead dead slow with the rudder turning you toward the dock. This will kick the stern out away from the dock.

Once clear, you'll be able to back with rudder amidships.

SITUATION 7:
Estimating Depth

During your three-week vacation you are cruising the northern part of Chesapeake Bay. You have studied the pilot books and charts and know that many of the tiny creeks and rivers you plan to explore are very shallow, requiring careful navigation if you are to avoid running aground.

On the third day out, while slowly proceeding up a creek on the eastern shore, your electronic depthsounder stops working. You are unable to repair it.

You do not want to return to port for repairs, but you know you must be able to read depths accurately during this cruise. How can you do this?

HERE'S WHAT I'D DO . . .

SITUATION 7 Recommended Solution

Fashioning your own lead line is the answer. Although it has its disadvantages, it is guaranteed to be accurate, exerts no power drain on your battery, and requires no maintenance. It has no moving parts, requires no through-hull fitting, and is rarely a target for boat burglars. One additional advantage is its ability to collect a sample of the bottom, improving your anchoring strategy.

The lead line itself is something of an ancient nautical work of art. A lead line can be bought at local ship chandleries in fishing ports, but you may be met with empty stares if you ask for one at a large modern marina store. You will probably have to make it yourself.

The weight is available in many chandleries. It can be had in sizes from two to 15 pounds. When selecting the weight, be sure that there is a shallow depression at the end opposite the line. It is this cavity which allows you to sample the bottom by arming it with cup grease, tallow, or soap. If this retrieval system brings up nothing, you are very probably over rocks or coral. If the bottom is soft, you may find it packed with sand, pebbles, or mud.

It is a good idea to prepare the lead line in the old-fashioned way rather than by simply attaching numbers indicating fathoms. This will enable you to take soundings in the dark and know by feel what the depth is. The traditional markings for lead lines are:

2 fathoms	two strips of leather
3 fathoms	three strips of leather
5 fathoms	white cotton rag
7 fathoms	red wool rag
10 fathoms	leather with hole in it
13 fathoms	three leather strips
15 fathoms	white cotton rag

17 fathoms   red wool rag
20 fathoms   piece of line with two knots

Be sure to use a piece of small diameter synthetic line which will not shrink or kink.

SITUATION 8:
Selecting the Proper Anchor

After a full day of cruising, you locate what looks like a perfectly protected anchorage in a small cove. Your chart of the area indicates that the bottom characteristics are "Co."

You are equipped with a 25-pound plow and a 35-pound yachtsman kedge with narrow flukes.

After stationing a crew member on the bow, you carefully motor into the cove, planning to let go the anchor when your depthfinder indicates a depth of three fathoms.

Which anchor do you elect to use and how do you use it?

HERE'S WHAT I'D DO . . .

SITUATION 8 Recommended Solution

The yachtsman kedge is the natural choice, since its narrow flukes will hook well in the coral. Your plow anchor would be inappropriate here since its designed to bury itself in soft sand or mud bottoms.

Certainly you should have three fathoms or so of chain at the anchor end of the rode. Coral will cut through nylon in a hurry!

Before you drop the hook, be sure to rig a tripping device, which may save you a lot of time later. Just attach a line to the anchor's crown (the "T" where the flukes are attached to the shank), and place a buoy at the other end. If a fluke becomes jammed in the coral, a sharp pull on the trip line should release the anchor.

Once your crew lets go, you'll want to let out about 150 feet of rode, for a scope of 8:1.

SITUATION 9:
Fire

You're on the third day of cruising along the coast, about 20 miles from the nearest landfall. It's a perfect day for sailing, Force 4 winds, and your sloop is steering herself on a reach. It's noon, and you figure a hot cup of soup will taste great.

Suddenly, your wife screams. You see flames, and for a moment you can't believe your eyes.

The galley is on fire! What do you do?

HERE'S WHAT I'D DO . . .

SITUATION 9 Recommended Solution

First, take stock of the situation. What's on fire? The galley, or the whole forward end of your boat?

Since the fire is isolated (for now, at least) in the galley, use your fire-smothering blanket. Place it over the flames. That will cut off the oxygen and stop the fire.

As soon as possible, cut off the galley fuel, using the remote valve.

If a fire blanket isn't available, use your carbon dioxide or dry-chemical fire extinguisher. You *must* have one close at hand in the cockpit. You've only got about ten~to~20~seconds of action with that extinguisher, so use it effectively.

If the fire gets out of control, maneuver the boat so as to minimize the effect of the wind on the fire. Prepare to abandon ship by gathering all the lifesaving devices. Signal immediately for help.

SITUATION 10:

Clawing Off a Leeward Shore

The coastline north of your home port is a ruggedly beautiful area of steep cliffs. In fair weather it is one of the coast's loveliest sailing spots, providing hundreds of little coves for anchorage.

Your cruise in your 30-foot sloop would not be complete without a few days here. You plan to head slowly along the coast before ending your vacation.

You've studied the pilot books and realize that this area is in direct line of the strong easterlies which sometimes blow in the area. You've also noted that there are no sheltering harbors along a long section of the coast.

As you reach along the coast on a port tack, you and your guests marvel at the unspoiled beauty only a mile off your starboard beam. Just as you relinquish the binoculars to one of the crew, a strong gust of wind heels you over and you quickly ease the sheets.

A chill runs through your body as you consider the possibility of weathering a gale off this rocky coast.

While contemplating the fact that there are no other boats in the area, you come close to being knocked down by a sudden strong puff. The sea to windward is now full of whitecaps and the wind is quickly building. As the wind begins whistling through the rigging, you realize that you may have to claw your way off this dangerous lee shore in Force 7 and 8 winds.

What's your strategy?

HERE'S WHAT I'D DO . . .

SITUATION 10 *Recommended Solution*

"Never skirt a leeward coast" is one of the best pieces of advice ever given to the sailor. But the fact is that cruising sailors—particularly those who generally sail coastwise—will often find themselves in just this situation. Realizing that it's best to avoid lee shores is important, but it's more critical to know what to do when the inevitable occurs.

Your ability to claw your way off a dangerous lee shore will depend on many things, but the two most important are the weatherliness of your boat and your knowledge of sail trim. Some hull designs, for example, are notorious for their poor windward performance. The traditional Colin Archer type with its long keel, pointed stern, and deep forefoot, does not do well into the wind and is often difficult to tack.

To determine your boat's capacity for working her way to weather when wind and seas increase must be a matter of experimentation. It's best done when you are in an area in which you can simulate a lee shore. Don't wait until your survival *depends* on your knowledge of your boat's weatherliness.

Although your boat's weatherliness must be learned through practice, managing sail trim is something to which you can productively apply theory. A cruising sailor, who is often quite unconcerned about the finer points of sail trim efficiency, draft position, and differential surface pressure, can learn a lot from the racing sailors about fighting off a lee shore. Like them, you'll find yourself trimming sheets constantly, heading off a bit in the strong gusts, and heading up during the lulls to get the best out of your boat.

The wind constantly changes direction and speed. Your skill in recognizing these changes and taking advantage of them could spell the difference between a pleasant day of sailing and disaster.

Before turning your attention to sail trim, however, you should immediately reduce sail, since the wind is now at Force 7. To keep an already strong weather helm from becoming a real backbreaker, reduce sail starting from astern. As you take some reefs in the main, you'll notice an immediate easing of the helm as the center of effort moves forward. Be sure the reduced main is properly balanced with a smaller headsail—one with a longish luff. Although you might be tempted to hank on your smallest headsail, it probably wouldn't provide enough drive to get you upwind.

Now that your rig is well-balanced for the job at hand, start thinking like a racing sailor who has half the fleet ahead of him. Live by the maxim "Distance to windward is everything." Keep in mind what makes the sails get you to windward: pressure differential. The main and jib must be curved, causing the air on the convex side to move faster than the air on the concave side. The resulting low pressure on the front sides of the sails is what moves you to windward.

In high winds like you're facing now, the amount of curve must be adjusted to control the increased forces on the sail. For the main, this means getting the foot and luff tension as tight as possible, flattening the sail to keep it from becoming over-powered. If possible, also move the boom outward by adjusting the traveller. This will reduce the tendency to heel and increase forward drive.

Tightening the jib luff is also extremely important for good windward performance. The jib's sheet leads can be adjusted fore and aft so that the tension on the leech and the foot is about equal. This will improve the shape of the sail and help you get more drive.

The wave action will be particularly uncomfortable near the coast, but it will ease considerably as you get away from the confused rebounding seas. The rougher the seas, the more important it will be for you to bear off a bit to keep your boat's speed up. Do not sheet the sails too tightly or head too close into the wind. Only if a particularly large sea approaches should you head directly into it. Immediately bear off. You must maintain steerageway; otherwise, you'll lose control.

Once again, think like the racing sailor. Watch the luff of your jib closely. If it begins to shake, you're pointing too high and certainly losing speed. Bear off a bit to keep the sails full.

When it comes time to tack, be sure you have enough boat speed to come around through the strong wind and the heavy seas. This maneuver can be so difficult that some sailors recommend jibing around instead. But in the gale winds you're faced with, you probably do not want to give up the distance a jibe requires, nor do you want to put that much pressure on your rig.

SITUATION 11:

Picking Up a Mooring with No Engine

You have had a fine day of cruising to a cove about 17 miles away. You have two guests aboard and are returning to port. The wind is Force 4.

When you test your engine a few hundred feet outside the harbor, it stops. As you attempt to start it again, you notice that your inflatable dinghy is making odd maneuvers behind you. It doesn't take you long to realize that about 20 feet of dinghy painter has wrapped itself around your propeller.

There is no chance of using your engine until someone dives to unfoul the mess. You will have to pick up your mooring, situated just 100 feet off the club's veranda, under sail.

What is your strategy?

41

HERE'S WHAT I'D DO . . .

SITUATION 11 Recommended Solution

Picking up a mooring under sail is like driving a car with no brakes. Consider the difficulty of stopping your car at an intersection precisely at the near side of a crosswalk without using the brakes.

Impossible? No. Difficult? Very.

There are two schools of thought when it comes to picking up a mooring under sail. One requires that you know with great precision how far your boat will carry upwind in various conditions with sails luffing. That this distance is a function of innumerable combinations of variables explains why so many attempts to "shoot a mooring" end in dropped boat hooks and flaring tempers.

The second school provides a more conservative approach, requiring that you maintain control of your boat by sailing it all the way to a mooring buoy.

It is the set of the sails which determines how much power, or drive, they have. And it is this drive which, for the most part, controls the speed of the boat. If you can control the speed of your boat under sail, you can make it stop at the mooring buoy.

Begin by approaching the mooring on a close reach. If you want to slow down, you can. Just luff the sails by easing the sheets or heading up into the wind. Conversely, if you want to increase your speed, you can trim sheets or fall off to leeward.

Although this method is much superior to the long head reach into the wind technique, you must be careful not to slow so much that you lose steerageway and control. The goal is to retain control as long as possible, stalling the boat's forward speed at the last moment. Done properly, this will place the mooring buoy at your bow ready for retrieval by your waiting crew.

As soon as your crew signals that the warp is through the mooring ring (not before), get the sails handed quickly lest the boat try to sail the warp out. If you miss the buoy, an event guaranteed to occur more than once, you may be in irons, head to wind with the sails flapping.

43

Let nature take her course by making some sternway, backing the jib, reversing rudder, and waiting for the sails to fill.

If you're faced with a situation where, due to other boats or moorings being in the way, you must approach your mooring from upwind, control can still be maintained. Use your headsail only—the main must be down—decreasing speed by easing the sheets. Try to run in with the wind on the quarter rather than dead astern to keep the jib from wrapping itself around the forestay.

If there is a tide running, things get a bit more tricky. If the wind and the tide are from the same general direction, you can sail up to the mooring, making adjustments to allow for the set of the current. If the wind and tide are opposed, you must plan on handing your mainsail before reaching the mooring, for the wind will be abaft your beam after you've secured, the force of the current being stronger than the wind once the sails are down.

Although you may not fetch the mooring the first time you try, practice will help you gain greater control over your boat in close quarters. The bonus is that you also learn a lot about man overboard maneuvering under sail, which can be far more critical than getting to a mooring the first time.

One final suggestion: Have your anchor at the ready while shooting a mooring. If things get really out of control, there's no need for bashing about the anchorage, damaging other boats and your ego.

SITUATION 12:
Running Inlets

It is the final day of your cruise and you are heading back to port. You want to make the 139-mile trip as quickly as possible since the charter on your 33-foot sloop ends in two days.

Your course is northerly, and off your port beam, the long straight beaches stretch along your route as far as you can see.

The wind, now up to Force 5, veers and becomes easterly. You are becoming increasingly concerned that those sweeping beaches have become a close lee shore.

Your boat is riding uncomfortably in the trough, and the seas are continuing to build. One of your guests loses his balance and crashes against the side of the cabin hatch. He winces in pain and complains of difficulty in breathing. Based upon your limited knowledge of first aid, you conclude that he has at least one broken rib.

Concerned about his injury, you decide to enter the next port, four miles up the coast. Quickly checking the pilot book, you find it says: "Could be dangerous to enter with strong easterly winds." The chartlet of the small port shows two parallel breakwaters jutting directly into the sea.

When the entrance comes into view, you can see that seas are breaking in the entrance. Deciding that running the inlet is a small price to pay for the security of the small marina inside, you start your approach.

What is your strategy for running the inlet?

HERE'S WHAT I'D DO . . .

SITUATION 12 Recommended Solution

The best strategy is to execute a 90-degree turn to starboard and get away from the breaking seas in that inlet.

Unless you are able to resist the desire to seek the shelter that seems "so near yet so far," your friend may require medical attention for much more than just a broken rib.

Sailboats, with their displacement hulls and small auxiliary engines, are great with plenty of searoom about, but they are complete hogs when it comes to close-in maneuvering in difficult conditions. Nowhere is this more true than when attempting to run an inlet with heavy, breaking seas.

In order to run an inlet successfully, you need power. Lots of it; enough to go fast enough to keep up with the waves. If you don't have plenty of power, your boat will be pooped by a breaking sea rushing up from behind, possibly causing a broach. Worse yet, if caught on the face of a breaking sea, a small boat could easily bury her bow and pitchpole end over end.

Those swells may be travelling from ten to twenty knots. It's obvious your boat would be overtaken by one or more of them if you attempted entrance.

If the tide is ebbing, you might have a chance to enter later. The rough seas will probably moderate when the tide turns. You could consider staying in the area, waiting for slack water and improved conditions. Then, if there are no breaking seas in the entrance, you might elect to go in. Everyone should wear life jackets and you should observe the seas diligently, attempting to predict whatever flat spots might occur. Even though it might look like a piece of cake, you'll be in for a short, but vigorous, roller coaster ride.

But if the seas continue to break, don't attempt entrance. Check your charts and pilot book for the nearest harbor which is safe to enter with strong easterly winds. Sure, it may be another day at sea or even two days, but at least you'll be able to enter port safely when you get there.

Meanwhile, you can administer first aid to your friend. In the case of a broken rib, it is nothing more than an elastic bandage placed around the lower half of his chest to restrict movement and relieve the pain.

SITUATION 13:

Buoyancy, Displacement, and Gravity

This weekend's cruise, with four guests aboard, has been perfect: a combination of fine weather, good companionship, and the satisfaction of knowing that you are introducing two of your friends to sailing for the first time.

When you and one of the novices are alone in the cockpit, he turns to you and says, "I'm very embarrassed about this, but I can't figure it out. What makes boats float?"

How do you answer him?

HERE'S WHAT I'D DO . . .

SITUATION 13 Recommended Solution

Although your friend's question sounds simple, many cruising sailors would have a difficult time answering it.

Three interrelated concepts explain why boats float: buoyancy, stability, and gravity.

First, consider buoyancy. Discovered by Archimedes, it is central to understanding why some objects can stay on the surface of the water and others quickly sink.

Only those objects which are designed properly will be supported by water. You can prove this, as Archimedes did, by using two lumps of soft copper. Fashion one into a box shape; just four sides and a bottom, like a barge. When placed in water, it will float. The other lump of copper will of course sink immediately.

The design of the first lump enabled it to displace an amount of water equal to its own weight. Therefore, the property of "buoyancy," which all fluids have, supported the box-shaped copper.

Stability was also noted by Archimedes in his experiments. Urns and vases, he observed, would fill with water as they bobbed to and fro, then sink. They were no longer able to displace an amount of water equal to their own weight. They weighed more, due to the water inside of them, but since their design was unchanged they were unstable. Consequently, they were unable to take advantage of the property of buoyancy.

To float indefinitely, a vessel must be designed to be stable—to remain "right side up." Archimedes accomplished this design when he attached a weight to the bottom of an urn. Its stability, although not perfect, improved very considerably.

Finally, gravity also helps to explain why boats float. Your boat has mass, and therefore is affected by gravity, a force which pulls it toward the center of the earth. It does not sink, of course, but only because it is designed to be buoyant.

Gravity also contributes to the boat's stability by tending to keep the keel in a downward position.

Tossing a Line

After two weeks of bareboating in the Caribbean, you've just entered your final port. You circle slowly, checking out the other boats while searching for a spot which will give you maximum maneuvering room. You intend to moor stern to the quay.

You locate a wide-open section and begin backing toward it. Your crew on the bow drops the anchor at your command, and tells you it is well set as the rode is played out.

A small crowd of tourists forms on the quay, evidently hoping for a good show. The maneuver is going well until the screw fouls in a piece of line and the engine stops.

You're about 30 feet from the quay. The engine will not restart. Your boat lies motionless in the water. Without diving in or using the dinghy, what's the best way to finish mooring?

HERE'S WHAT I'D DO . . .

SITUATION 14 Recommended Solution

Since you are only 30 feet from the quay, the best solution is to throw a mooring line to one of the persons on the quay.

Some sailors may resort to swimming a line ashore. Others may board the dinghy and row the line to the bollard. Still others will pick up a confused bird's nest of twisted rope and hurl the whole mess in the general direction of the quay hoping that it will somehow unravel in midair.

Knowing how to heave a mooring line properly is the only answer!

Doing it right is simple, but most cruising sailors don't know how. Like most things, heaving a mooring line correctly is 90 percent preparation and ten percent doing. Coiling the line correctly is the key to the whole operation.

The first thing to do is to put a small bowline on one end of the line and slip this over your left wrist. (If you are left-handed, reverse the hands throughout the instructions below.) This little trick ensures that you'll retain at least one end of the line on the boat.

Then, with the right hand, measure out about an arm's length of line. Loop that back over your left hand, just laying the succeeding loops into the flat of your outstretched left hand. Naturally, you'll want to give the line a twist for each loop to prevent it from kinking and twisting. If your mooring line is made of braided rope, it will invariably form figure eights instead of loops—nothing to worry about.

How many feet of line do you need? Well, you estimated you were 30 feet off, so you'd best get at least 36 feet looped in your left hand. Figure about a yard per loop, so that's 12 loops in total.

Before you make your heave, put half the loops into your right hand —being sure you remove them in reverse order. You should end up with the 12th, 11th, 10th, 9th, 8th and 7th loops in your right hand and the remainder in your left. This is highly critical! If the loops do not pay out in the reverse order that you put them on your left hand, you'll be tying airborne knots.

54

Now, stretch out your *left* arm toward the quay, keeping your palm open. Heave the six loops with your right hand. The remaining loops in your left hand will feed out smartly.

Finally, just ask the people on the quay to secure the line to a bollard. *You'll* haul your boat in, not them!

SITUATION 15:

Compensating for Current

Your destination this leg of your cruise is a small port 102 miles distant. Using your course plotter, you determine that the true course to your target is 090 degrees.

You've never had to deal with current before, but the situation will be different today. Strong north winds over the past few days have affected the water in the channel.

Your pilot book tells you that the offshore current sets in a general SSW direction at a velocity of one-half to two knots. This current is affected by the wind.

You figure you'll average about 4 knots on this crossing. Based on the pilot book's statement regarding the current, you estimate its drift at two knots and its set at 202 degrees true.

What course do you steer to make port?

HERE'S WHAT I'D DO . . .

SITUATION 15 Recommended Solution

Most of the time, getting a small boat from point A to point B is simply a matter of putting the bow in the direction of your destination and getting under way. If the water you're travelling in doesn't move much during the passage, this approach should work pretty well.

Introducing the factor of water which refuses to remain stationary, however, makes for a more complex problem. Handling situations like this requires the use of a current triangle, sometimes called a vector diagram. There's no math involved. All you need is a pencil, a course protractor, a pair of dividers, and paper.

The important thing to keep in mind about a current triangle is that the length of each of its sides represents *speed* in knots as well as the more obvious factor of *direction*. The direction part is easy—you just lay the lines off using the course plotter or protractor. For speed, however, you'll want to select a convenient linear scale which will be the same for all three sides of the current triangle—one knot must be the same length on each of the three sides.

The completed triangle will show the following: On one side the estimated set and drift (direction and speed, respectively) of the current. On another, your boat's speed and course through the water. The third side will represent the boat's track, or direction and speed made good relative to the earth. Since each side is dual purpose—showing both direction *and* speed, every current triangle (when completed) contains six pieces of information. Normally, you'll know, or be able to estimate, four of these six. You'll be solving the triangle for the other two.

In preparing for your cruise across the channel, the four elements which you know are:

1. The set (direction) of the current—you've estimated that to be 202 degrees true.
2. The drift (speed) of the current—once again an estimate: two knots.

3. The "track" direction. This is simply the true direction to your destination. It is 090 degrees true.
4. The speed of your boat through the water—you're figuring on an average of four knots.

The two "unknowns" in this situation—the reasons for getting so involved in triangle-drawing—are (1) the true course to steer and (2) the speed of the "track," i.e., your actual speed over the ground.

Now you can begin to draw the current triangle. First, indicate a "north" on the diagram, as shown in Figure A. Lay off a line from the origin which will represent the current's direction and magnitude—202° and two units long (for two knots).

Another known element is the direction to your destination. Lay this off from the same origin—a direction of 090°. At this point, however, you do not know how long to make this line, since you do not yet know your actual speed over the ground. Consequently, it will be an indefinite length for the present.

The final known element is your estimated speed through the water, four knots. Set your dividers for a magnitude of four knots using the same scale you used for the current's drift. Then, swing an arc from the end of the current line which intersects the line representing the actual direction to the port. Finally, draw the third side of the current triangle, running from the end of the current line to the point of intersection.

The solution for the two unknowns is now straightforward. Using the course plotter or protractor, determine the direction of the line you have just drawn. This direction is the course (true) you should steer. Like all true courses, it needs to be corrected for variation and deviation. In order to avoid a solution which is the reciprocal of the course you really want, remember this important rule: The arrows representing motion of the current and the motion of the boat through the water will always have a "head-to-tail" relationship (i.e., the head of one touches the tail of the other). Then, measure off the number of units between the origin and the point at which the arc intersected the line representing the direction to the port. The number of units is equal to the actual speed you'll make over the ground.

Simply stated, this current diagram has told you how much to "crab" into the current so that it doesn't set you too far south. You can now estimate your time of arrival since you now know your actual speed over the ground.

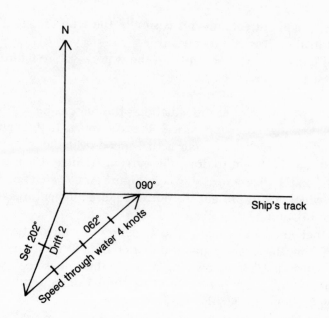

N

090°

Ship's track

Set 202°

Drift 2

062°

Speed through water 4 knots

Figure A

SITUATION 16:
Rafting

The fleet regatta was a big success. Your local club finished well in the final day's races and you are headed, with 32 other boats, to the club's favorite anchorage.

You arrive a little late, and find the small cove full of boats: standing room only. Eager to join in the festivities, you pick out the smallest raft of boats, a seven-boat "lash-up," and begin to make your approach. Your friends, who are by now deeply involved in swimming and the throwing of water-filled balloons, wave and invite you to join their raft. Seems easy enough to you, even though this is the first time you've rafted-up.

What's your plan?

HERE'S WHAT I'D DO . . .

SITUATION 16 Recommended Solution

The first thing to think about when planning to raft-up is to arrange to have the largest boat go in first and drop its largest anchor. Then each of the smaller "guest" boats can proceed alongside. Decide on which end of the nest to tie up. This should not just be a matter of where your best friend is located, but also how you can best balance the raft around the anchored boat. If, for example, there are four boats of similar size to port of the anchored boat and only three to starboard, you should tie up on the starboard side.

Get plenty of fenders over to port, then make your approach with just enough speed to maintain rudder control. Once you've approached on a parallel course and maneuvered to a position five to ten feet off the boat to port, heave over bow and stern lines. As an alternative, you can approach the other boat's bow at about 45 degrees and pass over the bow line first.

Be sure to stop your engine smartly, thus avoiding the potential embarassment of carrying everyone off and tripping the only anchor holding things together.

Once secured with bow and stern lines, position the boat so that your mast and spreaders are *not* in line with those of your neighbor. Otherwise, damage may be done when the boats roll. Spring lines will be necessary to maintain this position.

Rafting is at best a tangle of lines and bashing about. The decision to remain in such a situation overnight should not be made lightly. Check the weather forecast. Even if it is *favorable*, leave! Relying on one anchor attached to a boat which is located three boats away from you makes little sense.

If, however, you do decide to stick it out till morning, consider having each of the outboard boats put out anchors, about 45 degrees outboard from your bows. If there's a significant increase in the wind or a shift, you'll have to break the raft up, but these additional anchors will stabilize things until the inevitable happens.

Sometimes, however, you will be rafted-up at a quay, a far less chancy way to spend the night. For one thing, you'll be able to put over lines to the quay fore and aft as well as bow, stern, and springs to the boat next to you. These long lines should pass *under* all intervening lines on their sometimes circuitous route to the bollard.

When you go ashore, don't climb through your neighbors' cockpits unless you must. Light-footedness across the foredeck is the accepted etiquette. Just try being inboard to a ten-boat lash-up some night while complete strangers march through your cockpit every half-hour or so, placing one foot in your still-warm hibachi and the other on your dog's left paw. Definitely attempt to arrive late, thereby assuring yourself of the preferred outboard position.

Order-of-departure the next morning makes for fine sport. Hoping that the raft is "combat-loaded" and he who is outboard will leave first is the height of folly. Someone near the center of things generally wants to be under way at first light, and this will require some major adjustments lest the raft come apart. The general rule here is to squeeze the early-riser out downwind, allowing the gap to close up fairly automatically. If he proceeds upwind, the lines will have to be handled much more smartly to keep the raft from collapsing.

Tuning the Rigging

You've just completed a week-long trip through some very scenic canals. Your 30-foot sloop is now moored at a small harbor on the coast. Your mast, which you unstepped before you entered the canals, protrudes at bow and stern, securely lashed to the jury-rigged supports you fashioned out of used lumber over two weeks ago.

You've persuaded the local yard to make its hoist available to you first thing in the morning.

Unfortunately, you were a bit rushed when you unstepped the mast, and forgot to mark the shrouds and stays. You've spent most of the afternoon sorting out a complicated mess of stainless steel. You also neglected to mark the turnbuckle screws for the right tension, so you'll have to tune the entire rig again.

There are no riggers available in the small port. How do you tune the rigging yourself?

HERE'S WHAT I'D DO . . .

SITUATION 17 Recommended Solution

For the racing sailor, tuning the standing rigging can be a most complex problem. What with flexible rigs, raked masts, and hydraulic tensioners, the subtleties of fine-tuning requires a healthy amount of aerodynamic engineering expertise.

The cruising sailor who's not overly concerned about reaching the next port in record time faces a much less demanding task.

Probably the most important thing for the cruising sailor to keep in mind is the need for fairly constant tension in the standing rigging. If the tension of your stainless steel wire rope is allowed to fluctuate, the risk of it weakening and parting increases rapidly.

After you've stepped the mast—preferably with no damage to the deck house—position it athwartships (in the plane which is perpendicular to the keel) by adjusting the upper shrouds.

A halyard can be used to help you get the mast perpendicular. When it is perpendicular, the distance from the masthead to opposing points on the toe rail will be equal port and starboard.

Fortunately, there's a widely accepted rule for tuning: The upper shrouds should have the greatest tension, followed by the forestay, then the lower shrouds, and finally the backstay.

Be sure that the mast has no curvature in it by sighting up the sailtrack. Curvature, if any, can be removed by a combination of adjustments to the forward and after shrouds, or the stays. But, be sure that opposing shrouds have *equal* tension.

It's also important that the forestay, while not as tight as the upper shrouds, be fairly taut, since any sag in the luff of the jib will materially affect your ability to sail to windward.

Once you've completed this in-port tuning, get under way and go to weather with the boat heeled about ten degrees. Now sight up the mast to see if there is any curvature and check the leeward shrouds —they should have just a bit of slack. If there's any curvature or too much slackness, make the necessary corrections by adjusting the appropriate turnbuckles. (Be sure they are the leeward turnbuckles when you adjust, however, since the threads may become stripped if you attempt adjustment while they are under pressure.)

When you've finished your test sail and are back in port, the fine-tuning completed, secure the turnbuckles with seizing wire or cotter pins. Finally, wrap some tape around them to reduce corrosion and protect sails from ripping.

SITUATION 18:
Man Overboard

You're planning to spend the long weekend gunkholing along the coast of a small island about 20 miles off the coast.

You are en route there now, 12 miles out, on a comfortable beam reach. The wind is beginning to pick up, however, and you estimate it at about Force 5 or 6. You have reduced sail by reefing the main and hoisting the working jib, but are still cracking along at a brisk speed, the rail dipping underwater every few minutes.

When your wife goes below to prepare appetizers you notice a twist in the boom vang. After securing the tiller, you head forward to unfoul it. As you lean over the starboard life line—too far out, you know—the life line parts. Although you don't believe this can be happening to you, you wildly claw for the broken life line as if you were falling off a cliff. Your right hand flails into the nearest stanchion, snapping your wrist. As you tumble over the side, your forehead smashes into the boom, and you momentarily lose consciousness.

When you regain your senses after a few moments in the chilly water, you see your boat 50 meters away, heading away from you. Your only thought: Can your wife bring the boat back? What actions should she take?

HERE'S WHAT I'D DO . . .

SITUATION 18 Recommended Solution

This is one time when practice drills at the beginning of the season will undoubtedly pay off. Too often, though, these drills are conducted on flat, boring days when there's not much else to do. And it's typical that the skipper—who's the most likely to go overboard on a small boat —is the only one who gets the training.

People normally don't go overboard on the flat calm days. It happens when the wind and seas whip up and things become chaotic. Your training needs to simulate these conditions, since there is little similarity between man overboard maneuvers conducted in Force 2 and Force 6 conditions. You should spend several days at the start of the season practicing man overboard recovery techniques; first under ideal conditions, and then in more difficult situations.

Here's what to do to ensure that you live to skipper again:

First, get a man overboard system in the water immediately. The system should include the following items, all attached to a common line: a horseshoe-shaped flotation device with a whistle attached, a small drogue to prevent the system from being swept away, a dan buoy (a bottom-weighted floating pole at least seven feet long with a large flag at the top), a strobe light, and a packet of dye marker. The dan buoy is *essential.* Your head is an almost invisible tiny dot from 50 meters away. Throughout the entire maneuver you, or the dan buoy, must be kept in sight.

Second, she notes and writes down (Scratch it in the brightwork with a winch handle if nothing else is handy!) the course and time when you did your somersault. This information will be necessary if she loses sight of you and the man overboard system, since she will want to steer a reciprocal course.

Third, she begins what is optimistically known as the "pick-up maneuver." A jibe is much faster to turn the boat, but in these Force 5 conditions she may elect to come about. If she knows how to get the engine started, now's the time to do it, making sure no lines are in the

71

water to foul the propeller. With the engine on, she'll be able to maneuver much more easily, and return to you in less time (your boat covers the length of a football field in one-half minute at six knots).

If she doesn't use the engine, she should let the jib stream free by releasing the sheets, and utilize the main to make her approach. If possible, she should haul down the jib *if* it can be accomplished from the cockpit (with a jib downhaul device).

Fourth, she begins the approach—just as if she were picking up a mooring. When not using the engine, heading back to you on a reach is best, since she'll be able to head up or fall off once she gets you in sight. She can flatten or luff the main for speed control. She should stop the boat on the windward side of you. This is extremely difficult due to the momentum of the boat, rather like getting a freight train to stop at a crossing without using any braking system—she'll literally be coasting in to you. (Here again, the engine is enormously helpful, if she can get it started.)

Fifth, once she is alongside, she should immediately get a line over to you, preferably the end of the main sheet with a large bowline in it. You can put this over your head and under your arms. Then the ladder should go over to ease your climb aboard. If she has any doubts whatsoever about your ability to help yourself aboard, she should inflate the life raft. You'll find it easy to clamber into, and it will provide a platform for transfer to the boat later.

SITUATION 19:

Doubling the Angle on the Bow

It's 10 P.M. on a moonless night and you are sailing in company with another sloop, heading toward your next port of call, which is just to the left around a prominent headland about five miles distant. You've been asked to lead the way in, since you have visited this port before, and your friend on the other boat is very concerned about the "rocks awash" and other dangers shown on the chart. They appear to extend out from the headland approximately one mile. The only navigational aid from which to take a bearing is the clearly visible flashing light high on the point.

Unfortunately your chart does not show the height of the light, so you cannot calculate the distance using the vertical angle technique.

You decide that you want to pass no closer to the headland than three miles when it is off your port beam.

How do you ensure that you come no closer than three miles to the point?

HERE'S WHAT I'D DO . . .

SITUATION 19 Recommended Solution

Since it's dark and there are rocks ahead, conservatism is the name of the game. But there's no need to come right 90 degrees. You've established a reasonable and prudent goal: to clear the point by three miles, giving you a safety margin of two miles from the shoal water.

Basic trigonometry (the mathematics of triangles) will help you avoid the danger. The concept is simply this: If you know any two angles of a triangle *and* the length of the side between them, you can calculate the length of the other sides.

In piloting, the technique you'll use is called "doubling the angle on the bow." It requires that you take two separate bearings on the lighthouse and calculate the intervening distance. You can use this technique to do two things. First, it will tell you how far you are away from the headland *at the time* of the second bearing. Second, it can help you to predict how far off the headland will be when you *pass it abeam.*

The technique uses isosceles triangles, in which two sides are of equal length. One side will be the distance you travelled between the two bearings (you'll calculate that using the formula "Distance = Rate × Time" or read it off your log) and the other side will be the distance to the lighthouse. Whenever you "double the angle on the bow," you construct an isosceles triangle. The side adjacent to the second bearing is always the same length as the side between the two bearings.

But, what about *predicting* the distance from the point when you pass abeam? Simple, if you rely on a special case of "doubling the angle," called the 30°/60° rule. Using your compass, note the time that the light bears *30 degrees* off the bow (relative bearing). Then, note the time that it bears *60 degrees* (also relative). Using your estimated speed and the time elapsed, calculate the distance travelled over the ground. This, of course, is the distance you are away from the point at the time you took the 60-degree bearing. Now multiply that distance by seven-eighths (a handy decimal equivalent is .8). The result

75

is the predicted range at which you'll clear the light abeam. Using the 30°/60° rule, you can estimate how close you will pass abeam of the headland. It is approximately seven-eighths of the distance you travel between the 30-degree bearing and the 60-degree bearing, indicated by points A and B, respectively, in Figure A.

Figure A

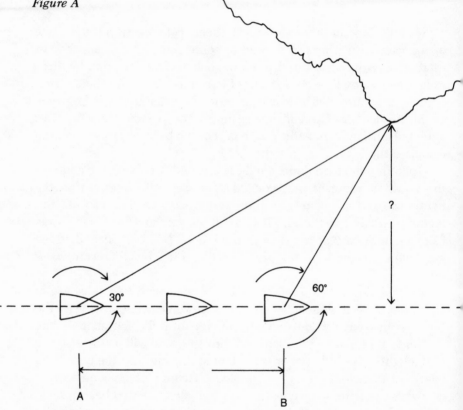

If it's less than three miles, come right to a new course which will give you the safety margin you want. If it's more than three miles, you can adjust to port.

Since you're using estimates, and there is danger ahead, remember two critical points. First, the estimated distance you have travelled is

76

over the ground, not through the water. If there's a current running, be sure and take that into consideration. Second, if you have no knot-meter, and are eye-balling your estimate of speed, guess on the *low* side. A mistake on the high side will give you a dramatically inaccurate predicted distance abeam.

SITUATION 20:

Correcting Weather Helm

You've recently purchased a 15-year-old double-ender—quite a classic little 8.5-meter wooden sloop. She surveyed very well, and now that you've refitted her with new stainless steel standing rigging and painted her topsides, you're on your first weekend trip.

You're cruising the Chesapeake, with a first day's run from Annapolis harbor over to the eastern shore, about 40 miles distant. Weather conditions have been quite good, with a pleasant Force 4 wind. Most of the trip so far has been a comfortable close reach.

Only one problem. After eight hours of sailing, you feel as though you've gone ten rounds with a world-class heavy weight boxer. Your arms are coming out of their sockets and your back is killing you. The boat's weather helm is much too heavy. Although you appreciate the margin of safety provided by a bit of weather helm, it's obvious that something is wrong with this boat.

How do you analyze this problem? What do you do?

HERE'S WHAT I'D DO . . .

SITUATION 20 *Recommended Solution*

First, the whole problem of too much weather helm resolves itself into two opposing factors, force and resistance.

All of the forces of the wind which operate on your boat can be thought of as centering on one spot called the center of effort above the waterline. This center of force meets resistance at the center of lateral resistance, a point below the waterline. It is the point around which your boat pivots. The interplay between these two points explains weather helm and lee helm.

Think about it. If the center of effort is *forward* of the pivot point, which way will the boat tend to rotate? Downwind, of course, causing what is known as "lee helm," a dangerous condition which can ultimately result in an accidental jibe as the boat spins away from the wind.

Conversely, if the center of effort is *aft* of the pivot point, the boat tends to round up into the wind. This is a nice safety feature, since if you leave the helm for any reason the boat will safely luff up into the eye of the wind.

But the problem you're faced with is too much weather helm. A bit is all right, but there's obviously too much safety factor in your boat.

The goal, then, is to bring the center of effort and the pivot point (center of lateral resistance) just a *bit* closer together. Not too much, of course, or you'll place the center of effort forward of the pivot point, resulting in lee helm. Remember, you always want the center of effort to be aft of the pivot point!

First, consider methods to move the pivot point a bit aft. Check the trim of your boat as she lies dead in the water on a calm day. Chances are she's "down by the bows," placing more surface under water forward. This, of course, moves the pivot point forward since there's more area underwater forward and less aft. You may be able to move some ballast aft, bringing the boat into trim and moving the pivot point aft.

Second, look at your boat's above water trim. The mast may be raked a bit aft. If you straighten it, the whole sail plan will move forward, causing the center of effort to move nearer the pivot point. Result: a reduction in weather helm. Or, you could increase the size of the headsail relative to the main. The same result: more effort forward, moving the center of effort closer to the pivot point. Or, adjust the trim of your sails. Let out a bit of main sheet while hauling in on the jib sheet for the same result: more effort forward, less aft. Remember, *the* purpose is to move the center of effort forward.

SITUATION 21:
Towing

You're returning to port under sail in your 30-foot auxiliary late one afternoon when you see a small sloop off the starboard bow. She's lying dead in the water. The U.S. ensign is flying upside down from her flag halyard, and the skipper is waving frantically, motioning for you to come alongside.

After checking your chart and depthmeter (you realize the sloop *may* be aground), you slowly approach. The skipper of the other boat shouts that his port spreader is broken and requests a tow into port, as he has no engine. You're willing to help him out, but what do you do?

It becomes obvious that you'll be totally in charge of the operation when he tells you that this is his "first time out!" There's a fair sea running with Force 5 winds. What's your plan?

HERE'S WHAT I'D DO . . .

SITUATION 21 Recommended Solution

After getting your sails down, begin to make your powered approach. Small boats have towed ones much larger than themselves under sail, but the close-in maneuvering should be done on the engine. You can proceed under sail power later.

Be sure to take plenty of time to get things sorted out aboard your boat. Ill-planned towing operations have ended in doing great damage to both boats, so don't rush it.

Use nylon for the towline. It's elasticity will enable it, instead of your deck hardware, to absorb most of the shock of the tow. Be sure to have a knife handy in case you need to terminate the tow in a hurry.

Your boat will steer as if a drunk were at the tiller if the towing point is anywhere aft of the rudder post, so forget attaching it to your stern bitt, samson post or cleat. Some sailors use one of their jib sheet winches, but you may not want these precious pieces of deck "gold" to take the punishment a tow can cause.

A better approach is to fashion a bridle out of another piece of heavy line. Secure it to the *forward* bitt, samson post, or cleat, running it back to the cockpit. Attach the tow line to this bridle with a bow line. This will prevent it from binding. Now coil the tow line carefully so it doesn't foul as you pay it out.

Secure the bitter end of the tow line to a float of some sort. The buoy you use for your anchor trip line will be perfect, or use an empty bleach bottle or seat cushion. Then you can float the tow line to the other boat, avoiding the embarassment of the inevitable failed heave.

Now make your approach from the distressed boat's stern. As you come alongside, stay a safe distance off, and inform the other skipper of your plans. Tell him to pick up the tow line with his boat hook as you drag it along his bow. Ask him to run it through a bow chock, around the base of his mast, out the other bow chock, and then secure it with a bow line in front of the bow.

As you start forward, pay out the tow line. While carefully tending it to prevent it fouling in your screw, maneuver so as to place its floating end at the bow of the other boat.

When the tow line has been secured, start the tow very, very slowly. Adjust the length of the line so that it matches the sea's wavelength. This will tend to place both boats on the "up" and "down" side of the seas at the same time, minimizing the damaging shock to the entire towing system which comes from your boat surging down a crest as the other fights its way up.

Finally, keep your crew away from the tow line as much as possible. Nylon gives no visual or audible warning when it approaches the breaking point, and the whiplash can have disastrous results.

Navigating in Fog

You've left your slip at Gashouse Cove on the south side of the entrance to San Francisco Bay, and have spent the day cruising Angel Island and the north side of the bay. It is 11:30 P.M. now, and you and your three guests are heading back across the bay. You have a 12-knot breeze off your starboard beam. The navigation lights on Alcatraz, which lies between you and the marina, are clearly visible, as are the lights of various towboats, barges, freighters and ferries.

Off your starboard beam, you can clearly see the Golden Gate Bridge.

The strong San Francisco tidal current is ebbing now, and you have used a vector diagram to adjust your course to compensate for the billions of gallons of water pushing you towards the bridge at a steady four knots.

Suddenly you hear the familiar sound of the two-tone foghorn at the north end of the bridge. You look west just in time to see the lights of the bridge disappear in a thick, fast-moving fog bank. The single-tone foghorn on the south tower of the bridge also begins to sound.

Thick fog quickly surrounds your boat—so thick that you can no longer see the bow pulpit. The lights on Alcatraz are now not visible, nor are the lights of any other object or boat.

Various sound signals join the two giant foghorns on the bridge. They seem to add to the confusion.

You also hear the "thrunk-thrunk-thrunk" throb of a large engine nearby. It comes closer and seems to come first from one spot, then another. You are relieved when the ominous engine noises recede into the background.

You realize that finding your way back to Gashouse Cove will be more difficult than usual in this fog.

What steps do you take to protect your boat and crew? What signals do you make?

HERE'S WHAT I'D DO . . .

SITUATION 22 Recommended Solution

Unless you feel it is absolutely necessary to get back to San Francisco, avoidance may be the better part of valor. A 180-degree turn may be appropriate.

The fog you've just penetrated is the typical Pacific Coast advection type, caused by the horizontal movement of warm ocean air across the colder waters near the coast. On a much-too-regular schedule, this coastal fog blows in on the onshore breezes in the afternoon or evening, and then recedes within 12 hours—only to return the next day like clockwork. At least you can figure on clear weather in the morning for another attempt at crossing the bay.

If you *do* decide to continue your trip across those very busy traffic lanes tonight, remember one thing: fog is a ventriloquist. It makes sounds appear to come *not* from their source, but from some other place. Consequently, sound signals in a fog bank can really deceive you.

Why, you wonder, do the only signals you're left with in a low-visibility situation seem so dangerous? Because the dynamics of their transmission vary greatly with changes in wind direction, the amount of water vapor in the air, and temperature. In addition, the quality of the sound itself is a key variable, for low-pitched fog signals travel much further than those which are high-pitched.

You rarely notice these anomalies on a clear day because our eyes tend to confirm or reject what our ears are trying to tell us. In fog, this visual source of confirmation is lost. Consequently, never rely solely on audible signals. They may well be coming from a different direction than the actual bearing of their source.

But how about getting safely across the bay this evening?

There are five things to remember.

First, since you will literally be sailing blind and "listening" your way across the bay, it's a good time to give yourself and your guests the added protection of life jackets. Although some sailors may think this premature, it definitely is *not*. At the least, they'll help keep you warm.

Second, it is time to hoist your radar reflector, if you haven't already done so. Although you are about to start making audible defensive signals yourself, there's little chance that the watch officers on large ships will be able to hear them *or* know which direction they're coming from. A good radar signal from your boat is your first line of defense.

Third, ask for volunteers. Somebody has got to assume the role of bow lookout. This person must report *anything* seen or heard. Even on a small boat, a bow lookout should be posted away from the noise and confusion of the cockpit.

Fourth, update your fix. It may be the last opportunity you will have before entering the fog bank.

Fifth, start using sound signals. If you are not equipped with a compressed air or gas cylinder horn, use the old-fashioned but thoroughly reliable lung-power type. If you are equipped with neither, make your signals with *anything,* remembering that low pitches carry further than high. Bashing away on a cast-iron skillet with your tool kit hammer is just fine in the absence of more conventional signals. Although other vessels may not be able to make a precise interpretation of the hammer-and-skillet routine, they'll at least know that something is out there.

Inland rules do call for a prescribed routine of fog signals for a sailboat under sail. These signals are designed to indicate your presence as well as your approximate course to anyone who's listening. There are three basic rules to commit to memory:

STARBOARD TACK	*One* prolonged blast at intervals not greater than one minute
PORT TACK	*Two* prolonged blasts at intervals not greater than one minute
WIND ABAFT THE BEAM	*Three* prolonged blasts at intervals not greater than one minute

You'll want to use your watch to be sure you are signalling at the right intervals and for the correct length of time (a prolonged blast is defined as four to six seconds in duration).

What do you do if you're under power? Simply sound one prolonged blast every minute. If a vessel is towing you'll hear one long blast followed by two short (one second) signals.

At anchor, the proper fog signal is a bell rung rapidly for about five seconds.

Successfully negotiating San Francisco Bay in a fog will provide you with a new appreciation of returning to home port. Upon arrival at Gashouse Cove, as you hand your sails and start the engine, you can be thankful that you had sail power out on the bay and were able to listen actively without the interference caused by an engine.

Heavy Weather Tactics

You are cruising to Catalina Island, 35 miles from your home port at Marina del Rey near Los Angeles. The weather is beautiful, so clear, in fact, that you have had the island in view since leaving port.

Your turn on the radio to check the hourly weather forecast. To your shock, the Coast Guard is predicting a severe Santa Ana condition—offshore winds which roar across the California desert, increasing speed as they funnel down the mountain passes to the ocean.

You are 20 miles out, with 15 to go to the island. The forecaster predicts winds of up to 60 knots.

Although it adds ten miles to your trip, you decide to run for cover on the lee side of the island. You figure that once you hook around the corner, you'll be able to ride out the Santa Ana in a small protected cove.

Knowing that the Santa Ana comes with little warning—no barometric change or cloud patterns—you review what you know about heavy weather tactics.

Assuming that the wind will progressively build to a full gale over a period of several hours, what's your plan?

HERE'S WHAT I'D DO . . .

If you're just a bit apprehensive about what the next few hours have in store for you, your guests, and your boat, well, that's positive. You may need the extra boost of adrenalin if the going gets particularly challenging. Replace fear with a plan of action and you'll find heavy weather sailing much more enjoyable. Review the plan with your crew now.

First, get all the gear lashed down. The dinghy probably needs some extra lashings, and all the miscellaneous junk in the galley must be securely stowed. If you end up with more things than you can cram into lockers, throw it all in a blanket and jam it into the head compartment somewhere.

Get some sandwiches made up and perhaps some coffee or soup stored in a thermos bottle. Drag out your foul weather gear and get it on. Do it now. Attempting to don foul weather gear in a wildly pitching boat is next to impossible. If forced below decks to change clothes, a good case of seasickness is guaranteed.

Get the life belts out and put them on now too. Since it has probably been months since you last even looked at a life belt, it may take ten minutes to sort out the knotted webbing.

Shut off all the sea cocks, including the one for the sink drain (at high angles of heel, it can siphon water into the cabin).

Update your position. Although you know where you are now by sight alone, visibility may become more limited as the storm approaches.

Keep looking aft, toward the mainland, waiting for the Santa Ana to approach. Far off in the distance, you'll see what looks like a frothy white line on the horizon. It's the front edge of the storm. Your first move should be to shorten sail immediately. Don't wait till the lee rail is buried constantly. Get the working jib or storm jib up and reef the main deeply. Try to keep the sail plan well balanced so that the center of effort maintains its position relative to your boat's pivot point.

As the leading gusts hit you, your boat heels over violently; she recovers nicely and you go onto a reach, heading north in order to clear the end of the island.

If the wind and sea conditions worsen considerably, you may want to heave to. This tactic is somewhat difficult in a fin-keel boat, but with your long full keel it may be a wise move.

To heave to, reef the main fully and replace the working jib with a storm jib. Then, back the jib to weather, sheet the main in as flat as possible, and lash the tiller down (rudder to windward so the boat wants to turn into the wind).

Heaving to will help you maintain your current position as the boat hobbyhorses back and forth onto and off of the wind. Her bow will keep pointing into the seas, providing a reasonably comfortable ride. While hove to, you can join your crew members below for some rest and a quick sandwich.

If conditions get much worse, and your boat is taking a real battering while hove to, you may consider lying ahull, with all sails down and the tiller lashed amidships. Many sailors, however, reject this tactic due to fear of capsizing when the waves are short and steep.

Since you have now cleared the tip of the island, you elect to run before the wind until you get in its lee. To do this, you should hand the main and rely solely on the storm jib to provide enough speed for control. You shouldn't steer directly downwind, but take the seas off the quarter to minimize the danger of pitchpoling or broaching to. If, as you surf down the front side of one of the swells, your speed becomes excessive, you should stream warps off the stern.

Nylon makes the best warp in this case since it is fairly elastic—its stretch will help to cushion the breaking effect. The best plan is to feed out the warp slowly, experimenting to get the right reduction in speed. Make the warp one large loop secured port and starboard on your boat's quarters.

This warp has two important benefits. First, its drag (controlled by the size and length of the line) will slow you considerably. Second, the warp will tend to break up the strong seas before they reach your stern.

You can also use a centuries-old technique to calm the seas. Spread oil on the water by using a specially designed canvas bag or simply a can of engine oil with a small hole punctured in it. Although this technique will not handle the really large seas, it will calm the waves considerably.

96

As soon as you're in the protected lee of Catalina, you'll find the seas will moderate very considerably; still, be wary of the strong gusts which will plunge down the deep canyons. They can really surprise you.

SITUATION 24:

Horizontal and Vertical Angles

Your goal for today's cruise is a small, circular island approximately 22 miles off the coast. It is steep-to, with almost vertical cliffs plunging into the sea on all sides. Your chart shows it to be three miles in diameter.

You have been under way three hours, and have the island clearly in sight. You have no speed or distance indicator aboard, nor do you have a compass.

How can you calculate the distance to the island?

HERE'S WHAT I'D DO . . .

SITUATION 24 Recommended Solution

You can easily determine how far away the island is. All you need is a ruler and a piece of string.

The geometrical rule which states that the sides of similar triangles are proportional will help you solve the problem, as shown in Figure A.

All you have to do is hold the ruler in your outstretched arm and sight across it toward the island, with the ruler in the horizontal position. As long as you know:

1. the length of the island in miles (you can get this from your chart);
2. the number of inches the island intercepts on your ruler;
3. the distance of the ruler from your eyes when you sight over it,

you can easily determine the distance to the island.

You already know the first of the three distances, the length of the island. From your chart, you have learned that it is three miles.

But what about the distance of the ruler from your eyes? That's what the string is for. Holding one end near your "sighting" eye, pull the other end out in your outstretched hand. Then, use the ruler to measure this distance in inches. (Once it has been used for this purpose, you can return the string to your bag of small stuff.) It's important to record this distance (maybe on the back of the ruler) so you can use it in the future.

Now, sight across the ruler toward the island, holding it parallel to the horizon, and measure the distance the island subtends on your ruler. This will be in inches, of course.

Let's assume in this case that you hold the ruler 30 inches from your eyes, and that the island subtends a distance of 10 inches on the ruler. You can now calculate the distance to the island by using the following easy formula:

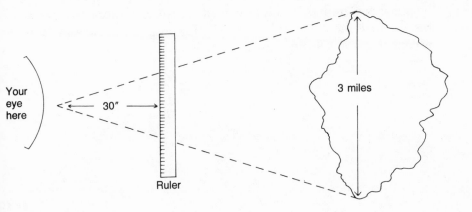

$$D = \frac{dL}{1}, \text{ where } D = \text{distance to island in miles;}$$

L = length of object in miles;
l = length object subtends on your ruler in inches;
d = distance of the ruler from your eyes in inches.

Substituting, you have:

$$D = \frac{(30'') \ (3 \text{ miles})}{10''}, \text{ or } D = 9 \text{ miles.}$$

You're probably wondering why this system works. It's simply understood if you take another look at Figure A, remembering the principle that the sides of similar triangles are proportional to each other. There are two similar triangles in the diagram. The larger, with points A, B, and C; the smaller with points A, b, and c.

Given this, the lengths of their sides are proportional. Thus,

$$\frac{D}{d} = \frac{L}{l}$$

Solving for D (distance to the island) which is, after all, the purpose of this exercise, you have:

$$D = \frac{dL}{l}$$

You can use this technique with vertical measurement as well as horizontal. All you must know is the height of some object (a light-

101

house, for example) and be able to see both its base and its top. Charts and light lists will often give you both the height above water and the height above ground. In this case, hold the ruler vertically to measure the distance the object subtends. The formula works the same way, except that you substitute heights for lengths.

SITUATION 25:
Thunderstorms

As an escape from the hot, muggy July weather, you are cruising along the coast in your 28-foot sloop.

At 1420, you notice some thunderclouds on the horizon. Since the wind is easterly and the clouds are to the west, you are not overly concerned. You are convinced that they will move further away as the afternoon progresses.

At 1600, you observe that, instead of retreating, the now towering cumulonimbus clouds are much closer to your position. They now obscure the sun and an eery calm surrounds your boat. Just as one of your guests remarks that something smells funny, you hear the rumbling of distant thunder and rain begins to fall.

Looking aloft through the slatting sails, you see menacing dark pouches on the underside of the clouds. You are 12 miles from the nearest port.

What critical mistake did you make about the nature of thunderstorms? How can you tell if the dangerous squalls which accompany thunderstorms will affect your boat? What do you do to ensure the safety of your boat and crew in this situation?

HERE'S WHAT I'D DO . . .

SITUATION 25 Recommended Solution

First things first. Reduce sail immediately. You can always hoist more sail if things aren't as bad as they look. Get everything loose tied down and don your foul weather clothing. Otherwise, you're in for a dousing of fresh and salt water!

Mistakes? Although you were correct in observing that the thunderclouds were to leeward of your position, you were incorrect in assuming that they would travel away from you. One of the treacherous things about thunderstorms is that they rarely, if ever, approach from windward. Oftentimes, they do come from leeward, against the prevailing wind.

It's not difficult, though, to determine the direction these storms will take. You can take bearings on them to see if they are moving toward you. The characteristic anvil top, when visible, acts just like an arrow. The storm will go wherever it points. Finally, the billowing "roll" cloud near the base of the storm is always at its leading edge—providing yet another indication of the storm's direction.

What about distance? Once you see the flashes of lightning, you can calculate it easily. Since you see the stroke of lightning almost instantaneously (it travels at the speed of light) but hear the clap of thunder some seconds later (it travels much slower, at the speed of sound), the interval between the two translates directly to distance. Simply allow five seconds to the mile. If, for example, an elapsed time of nine seconds occurs between the time you see the stroke of lightning and hear its thunderclap, the storm is 9/5 or 1.8 miles away.

That ghostly calm you're now in can tell you a lot about the severity of the coming storm. The longer it lasts, the more violent the storm will be. Whatever you do, don't make the all-too-common mistake of misreading this temporary lull and shaking out reefs.

One thing you probably do not need to worry about in this storm is waves. Thunderstorms rarely last long enough to raise destructive seas. But you do need to be concerned about very strong, gusty winds.

That the rain started *prior* to the wind is a danger signal. The following verse emphasizes that storms in which rain comes before the wind are the most violent:

> If the wind before the rain
> You may soon make sail again.
> If rain before the wind
> Top sails lower and halyards mind.

An early warning signal for approaching thunderstorms is your entertainment radio. That disturbing static which is so frequently a part of summertime listening is caused by electromagnetic activity such as lightning. If you are an FM fan, however, you'll need to tune in to the AM band once in a while. The modulated frequencies of the FM band are designed to filter out static.

The nature of the clouds themselves can tell you something about the strength of the storm. Take a look at their edges. If they are fluffy or loose, the storm will be weak. Conversely, if they are hard and solid, beware. Those ugly dark pouches you see on the undersides of the clouds are sure signs of a violent storm with high winds.

Finally, that unusual smell your guest noticed is not the smell of fear. It's simply ozone, a three-atom form of oxygen. Normally present in smoggy environments, it's also manufactured through the ionization of the atmosphere which occurs during thunderstorms.

Basically, there are only two types of thunderstorm activity—"air mass" and "frontal." The air mass storms are caused by warm air thermals rising into colder air. They are usually short-lived; you have probably observed their build-up along the coastline on hot, muggy days.

Frontal storms are usually more violent, particularly if they accompany a cold front. Fortunately, a quick check of the weather map will let you know if a frontal system is approaching your area. If a cold front is in the vicinity on a hot, muggy summer day, it's probably a good idea to stay in port.

While waiting for the storm to abate, don't feel too lonely. You've simply been caught out in one of the thousands of thunderstorms which occur each day all over the world. It's as much a part of sailing as pleasant anchorages and fair winds.

SITUATION 26:
Estimating Wind Speed

Since you've started cruising, you've become a student of the weather. You know how to swing a sling psychrometer and you know the difference between altostratus and cirrocumulus.

On board, you're equipped with an electronic anemometer, barograph, thermograph, and wind direction indicator.

While on a four-day crossing, your entire electrical system shorts. You control and stop the ensuing fire, but your 35-foot sloop's power system will be out until you can make repairs in port.

On the third day, the weather begins to deteriorate. You'll have to use your meteorological knowledge, since you cannot receive the radio weather reports.

What techniques can you use to determine actual wind speed and direction in the absence of any instruments?

HERE'S WHAT I'D DO . . .

SITUATION 26 Recommended Solution

There's no need to get upset about the lack of instrumentation. Even if the anemometer and wind direction indicator were working, you'd still have to figure out the *true* speed and direction of the wind.

Your instruments give you information about the apparent wind. This may differ, sometimes substantially, from the true wind, because your boat is moving through the air mass. Only when you are at anchor are the apparent and true wind the same.

This becomes clearer when you realize that you feel a breeze on your face when you are motoring in a dead calm. What you feel is of course apparent, not true, wind.

Wind direction can fool you too, since your boat's motion through the air seems to "bend" the direction of the wind.

Many cruising sailors do not have the instrumentation necessary to correct apparent wind to true wind. You'll have to rely on some methods used by sailors for hundreds of years.

One of the best known systems for estimating the true speed of the wind is the Beaufort scale. It has been in use since 1838, and is based primarily on observations of the state of the sea. Figure A summarizes the levels on the scale.

Many cruising sailors have difficulty with the Beaufort scale, particularly when it comes to discerning the differences between sea states. For example, it is very difficult to tell the difference between "moderately high waves with crests breaking into spindrift" and "sea heaping up with white foam."

The Navy has added a number of useful windspeed indicators which do not rely solely on observations of the sea state. They are shown in Figure B.

One very practical way to estimate the true wind speed is to be sensitive to the behavior of your boat when sailing to windward. If your boat is an average cruiser, you'll be able to beat to windward in

WIND SPEED	OBSERVATION
Less than 1 knot	Calm; smoke on land rises vertically
1–3 knots	Smoke drifts from stacks on land
4–6 knots	Wind is felt on face
7–10 knots	Wind extends light flag
11–16 knots	Wind raises dust, loose papers
17–21 knots	Wind snaps flags briskly
22–27 knots	Whistling in rigging
28–33 knots	Inconvenience in walking
34–40 knots	Wind generally impedes progress

Figure B

wind speeds up to about 35 knots. With stronger winds, you will no doubt find that impossible and will have to heave to or run.

The *direction* of the wind must also be determined. One simple way is to observe the direction of the smaller wavelets. They generally move with the wind. Or, if the wind is more than twenty knots or so, you'll be able to see the streaks that the Beaufort scale relies on. They are very clear indicators of wind direction. Both of these observations will give you a sense of the true direction of the wind, since they are unaffected by the motion of your boat.

Apparent wind direction can be estimated by watching your boat's flags. Once you've noted it, though, you may want to convert it—and the apparent wind speed—to true values.

There are at least four ways to do this. Three, however, are immensely time-consuming without a specially programmed computer. The one simple approach is the vector diagram, requiring only dividers, paper, pencil, and a course protractor. The steps are easy.

Starting at any origin point, draw a line toward the direction the apparent wind is coming from. Since vectors always show both direction and magnitude, the length of this line will represent also the apparent wind speed, to whatever scale you care to select.

If the apparent wind is on your port side, be sure that the first vector line heads off to the left of the origin. Conversely, it should go to the right if the apparent wind is on your starboard side.

Next, draw a vertical line down from the end of the vector. Its length represents your boat's speed through the water in the same scale units as the first vector.

Beaufort Scale

KNOTS	DESCRIPTION	SEA EFFECTS	BEAUFORT FORCE
0–1	Calm	Sea like a mirror	0
1–3	Light air	Ripples with appearance of scales; no foam crests	1
4–6	Light breeze	Small wavelets; crests of glassy appearance; not breaking	2
7–10	Gentle breeze	Large wavelets; crests begin to break; scattered whitecaps	3
11–16	Moderate breeze	Small waves; becoming longer; numerous whitecaps	4
17–21	Fresh breeze	Moderate waves, taking longer form; many whitecaps; some spray	5
22–27	Strong breeze	Larger waves forming; whitecaps everywhere; more spray	6
28–33	Moderate gale	Sea heaps up; white foam from breaking waves begins to be blown in streaks	7
34–40	Fresh gale	Moderately high waves of greater length; edges of crests begin to break into spindrift; foam is blown in well-marked streaks	8
41–47	Strong gale	High waves; sea begins to roll; dense streaks of foam; spray may reduce visibility	9
48–55	Whole gale	Very high waves with overhanging crests; sea takes on white appearance as foam is blown in very dense streaks; rolling is heavy and visibility reduced	10
56–63	Storm	Exceptionally high waves; sea covered with white foam patches; visibility still more reduced	11
64–118	Hurricane	Air filled with foam; sea completely white with driving spray; visibility greatly reduced	12–17

If you are sometimes amazed at the difference between reported wind speed and your impression of it a deck level, this may be because the reported speed is observed ten meters above sea level. At that height, the wind is generally one-third stronger.

Figure A

Finally, join the lower end of the second vector to the origin. The direction of this line away from the origin gives you relative wind direction. Analogous to a relative bearing, it must be corrected to true.

Simply add the relative direction to your boat's heading to find true direction. Don't forget to factor in corrections for variation and deviation, just as you would when converting a relative bearing to a true bearing.

The true wind speed is shown by the length of the third vector, in the standard scale units, of course.

An example will help to make this clear. Assume that you are on a true course of 010 degrees and your speed is 7 knots. The apparent wind is 35 degrees off your port bow. Observing the state of the sea and your boat's flags, you estimate the apparent wind speed to be 25 knots.

Figure C shows the three vectors. The first, at an angle of 35 degrees to the left of the origin point, represents the apparent wind's direction and speed. The vertical vector, which is seven knots "long" in standard units, represents your boat speed. The third vector provides the solution when it connects the bottom of the boat speed vector with the origin. Just measure the angle with your course protractor and the length (in standard units) with your dividers.The true direction of the wind is calculated by adding the relative direction to your course:

$$313° \text{ relative wind direction}$$
$$+\underline{010°} \text{ your course}$$
$$323° \text{ true wind direction}$$

True speed, measured off in standard units with your dividers, is 20 knots.

With a little practice, using the vector diagram becomes very simple. For most, it's far easier than the three alternatives: Table 10 in *Bowditch,* the U.S. Weather Bureau's Form 1209, or the chart produced by the Oceanographic Office.

There are three commonsense rules to remember when using the vector diagram to correct apparent wind to true wind:

1. The true direction is always on the same side of the bow as the apparent.

2. True wind speed is greater than apparent when the apparent direction is abaft the beam.

112

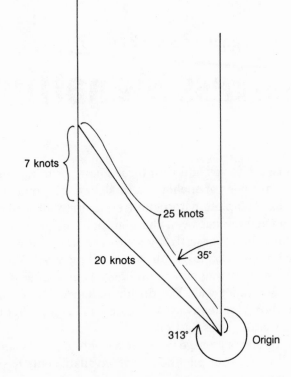

Figure C

3. True wind speed is less than (or equal to) apparent when true direction is forward of the beam.

There is one thoroughly reliable way to discover true wind direction, when you are close enough to port to observe the sea gulls. They invariably perch facing directly into the wind, making a handy automatic wind direction indicator when maneuvering in close quarters.

113

SITUATION 27:
Distress Signalling

For the past two days you and your three guests, cruising some islands off the coast, have been at anchor in a small bay. It's a miniature South Pacific paradise complete with palm trees, coral reef, and clear blue water. The anchorage has been the high point of the cruise.

This morning, however, a strong southwesterly is blowing directly into the anchorage. Coming with it is a strong swell. You hear the sounds of engines starting and chain being hauled in as many of the other yachts get under way. You decide to leave also and head for a protected harbor 26 miles away. You figure you can anchor there and take on water and necessary stores.

En route, you spot a passage between a steep-to small island and the mainland. Although your pilot book says "available only to small craft with local knowledge," your chart clearly shows a four fathom depth in the center of the channel. Since the shortcut takes ten miles off your trip distance, you change course.

While taking echo soundings as you enter the channel, your boat strikes an isolated submerged rock. You quickly get the sails down and rush below to assess the damage. You are startled to discover that seawater is now above the cabin sole. As you start your electric bilge pump, your boat strikes the rocks again and you hear the awful crunch that means even more damage.

Your guests are panicky now, and you've told them to get their life jackets on. Unfortunately, you have no life raft or dinghy. As the sun has set and the seas are rough, you realize that their lives may be in danger.

In the distance, you see the lights of some fishing boats. They are quickly heading away from your position and have not seen you.

As you switch on your radio, which is fortunately still working, one of your crew yells that the bilge pump has clogged.

How do you get one of those fishing boats to help you?

HERE'S WHAT I'D DO . . .

The word "distress" has a very special meaning to sailors. It translates to "serious or imminent danger requiring immediate assistance."

Although too many sailors cry wolf all too frequently for such non-distress situations as running out of fuel or being lost, the word aptly describes your situation. Now is the time to use every distress signal possible to attract the attention of one of the passing fishing boats.

Start with your radio, using emergency frequencies which are reserved specifically for emergency calls. Remember, though, that you can use any frequency for this purpose if the primary frequencies are not bringing help.

Although you may want to rush it, and your voice may be several octaves higher than normal, speak slowly and clearly. Repeat the word "Mayday" three times. Coming from the French *m'aider,* it means "help me," and is universally recognized. This begins the distress call.

Then, give the name of your boat and its call sign three times. If your radio is equipped with a two-tone alarm signal, transmit it for one minute before beginning the voice call.

The distress message itself begins by once again repeating the word "Mayday" three times, followed by the name and call sign of your boat, its position, and the details of the situation.

You can also transmit the letters "S O S" in Morse code over your radio. They are understandable in almost every language. The signal can also be sent by masthead light or foghorn. The letters were selected in 1908 not because they stand for "Save Our Souls" or "Save Our Ship," but for their easily recognized code equivalents (– – –/ . . . /– – –).

While attempting to get a response by radio, you should start using other distress signals as well. Red flares have long been the standard for distress signalling and are available in two distinctly different types. One, the parachute flare, goes as high as 1200 feet and if low cloud cover doesn't interfere, can be seen for many miles. The other, showing red stars at lower altitudes, can be used when there's cloud cover.

If you and your crew have not taken the time to learn how to use pyrotechnics by studying the label instructions, you should. In a distress situation, without light, it is difficult to study the directions carefully. Flares exploding at the wrong time, or in the wrong direction, have been known to set boats afire. They must be handled carefully, stored dry, replaced in accordance with directions, and their use mastered *before* a crisis occurs.

Beside the radio and flares, you can use your foghorn to make an audible distress signal. Sound it as continuously as possible.

In daylight hours, your flag may be a useful distress signal, if other craft are close enough to see it. A knotted flag is an ancient signal of distress, as is the ensign hoisted upside down. Beware of this last technique, particularly in foreign waters, where local boat operators may not recognize that your flag is inverted.

One of the newest international distress signals is a special 45" × 12" orange rectangular flag with a black 18" square and ball printed on it. This flag is similar to the old "distant signals" used by ships to relay messages when they were too far away from each other to see the color of the normal signalling flags.

In the absence of a special flag, a piece of red material tied to an oar or boat hook and waved slowly back and forth can be effective.

The official rules for distress signalling still include such odd things as setting fire to a barrel of tar or oil, but for many cruising sailors this would turn an already difficult situation into a holocaust. Best limit yourself to hand-held orange smoke flares.

A distress situation is one of the times when doing what comes naturally may well bring help. Waving your arms is an acceptable and widely used distress signals. Be sure to wave them slowly, raising and lowering them repeatedly over your head.

As you see the last fishing boat make a turn to port and head directly towards your position, you'll be thankful that you were familiar with the sailor's last line of defense: distress signalling.

Joining Two Lines Together

You're moored stern to the quay in a small port on the East Coast. The sea wall, a structure over 30 feet high, is on the far side of the quay.

Your pilot book tells you that the holding ground in the harbor is not good, so you have put out all your anchor chain forward with your Danforth anchor.

Although there is usually a westerly breeze in the afternoon, today easterlies have been steadily increasing. It is now blowing 30 knots and the barometer is falling.

The word among the other yachting people tied alongside you is that the weather will worsen, and it will put the quay to leeward.

You quickly decide to warp out away from the quay about 15 feet (you'll use your dinghy to get ashore). Once this is accomplished, you intend to set your second anchor for additional protection.

When you begin to get the anchor and tackle ready, you discover that you have only 50 feet of ⅝-inch-diameter nylon line. Not enough, really, to provide the scope you want for the coming storm.

However, you also have 60 feet of ⅞-inch Dacron line. You figure the two pieces of line together will be a long enough rode for the second anchor.

What's the best way to join them together quickly?

HERE'S WHAT I'D DO . . .

You may be tempted to use the simple square, or reef, knot for this, but don't. It wasn't intended for anything but small-size line, and *certainly* not for mooring warps of unequal sizes!

The sheet (or becket) bend is the ideal knot for this application.

Start just as if you were tying a square knot. Use the old adage "right over left, then left over right" to get started. Remember, a square knot will become a very dangerous *slip* knot if the ends are on opposite sides of the line when you're finished! Another mnemonic device, "secure if same," will prevent you from making this mistake. Combined, they'll keep you from committing a hugely embarrassing marlinspike sin: the granny knot.*

Once you've loosely formed the two loops of the square knot, remove one of the ends, and bring it under itself (see Figure A).

The sheet bend (also called the netting knot, mesh knot, or weaver's hitch) will rarely slip, even though the two lines you've joined together

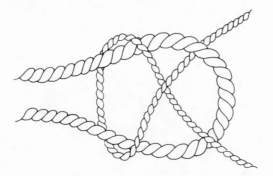

Figure A

*This infamous knot is mentioned in the 1867 edition of Smyth's venerable *Sailors' Wordbook*. The unliberated Mr. Smyth reports that "Granny's bend . . . is a term of derision used when a reef knot is crossed the wrong way, so as to be insecure. It is the natural knot tied by women and landsmen, and derided by seamen because it cannot be untied when it is jammed."

are of different sizes. But in this situation, you'll want maximum security. You can do two things to make the sheet bend even more sturdy.

First, you might consider stopping down both of the free ends. This will keep the knot from working itself loose as the surging power on the anchor line alternately stresses the knot. Secondly, you can "double" the knot, making it a double sheet bend, as shown in Figure B.

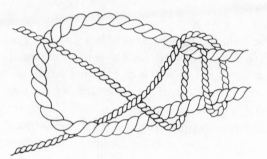

Figure B

Determining if the Anchor Is Dragging

Like many sailors, you enjoy getting away from crowded marinas and anchoring in the small coves which are located along the coast.

You have carefully studied the techniques for anchoring and have practiced conscientiously. But whenever you are anchored overnight, you are very concerned about dragging while you sleep. You have never weathered a blow at anchor, so you lack confidence in your anchoring system.

What are the techniques you can use to determine if your anchor is dragging?

HERE'S WHAT I'D DO . . .

SITUATION 29 Recommended Solution

The most certain way to discover that you're dragging anchor is that abominable crunch that comes when keel touches rock. To avoid this extreme approach to the problem, some fairly basic and quite creative solutions have been developed by cruising sailors.

Probably the most noticeable—and immediate—signal that you may be dragging anchor is the sound of increased wind and a changing motion in your boat. If you are one of those very sound sleepers to whom these signals of danger are reminiscent of being rocked in your cradle, you'll require something rather more alarming. Once you have developed confidence in your anchoring system, you'll be one of the few sailors who can get a good night's sleep while the wind tears at your rigging.

Almost always, when a boat drags as the wind and seas build, her heading will change considerably. An old-fashioned "tell-tale" compass—modernized perhaps by using an inexpensive runabout compass or hand-held job—will enable you, during one of your wakeful moments, to see whether or not your boat's heading has changed.

Another approach, still requiring you to wake up on a regular basis, is cross-ranges. These lines of position are so simple they do not even require the use of your compass. The difficult part, though, is finding two pairs of immobile objects on the shore which (a) will remain sufficiently lighted throughout the night and (b) are far enough away that the normal swinging of your boat does not substantially change the bearing of the two ranges. If you cannot establish ranges and instead rely on bearings on single objects or lights, be sure to record the compass bearing, as the normal swing of your boat will make relative bearings unusable.

If you go to bed before darkness sets in—a distinct possibility for cruising sailors during long summer days—you'll find that the seemingly familiar topography looks more like a moonscape at two in the morning. Either stay up till it gets dark or try to figure out what things will look like when there's no light. A full moon always helps in these situations but of course cannot be relied upon.

A creative approach to the problem of dragging when an audible alarm type depthsounder is available is to set it for the depth you want once you've settled into your anchorage for the night. If your boat, through dragging, moves toward the dangers of the beach, the audible alarm will sound. Although this technique is used by cruising sailors, it has two distinct disadvantages. First, the fathometer exerts a substantial drain on the electrical system if left to run all night, and secondly, it will not alert you if you are dragging toward deeper water or quickly shoaling rocks.

Many cruising sailors know that a drift-lead can be rigged after anchoring. All you have to do is lower a length of small line with a good heavy fishing weight at one end once you've anchored. Leave a bit of slack in the line. If you should drag, the weight at the end will pull the line taut—proof positive that you're dragging.

A wake-up alarm can be rigged by adapting an ordinary household doorbell to the system. Set it up so that it is powered by two flashlight batteries and rings when the pull on the lead line closes the contacts.

Surely one of the most necessary pieces of equipment if you decide to do much anchoring overnight in small coves is a really good spotlight. This does not have to be a chrome monster mounted on your cabin roof. There are plenty of superb 300,000-candlepower portable lights available which you can use with your boat's electrical system. A regular flashlight simply will not do! When you use one of these powerful lights, be sure you do not destroy your neighbors' night vision. They may be struggling to see what is going on too.

Even with the most elaborate drag alarm system, you will probably end up like most sailors who find themselves anchored off a lee shore. You'll stand an anchor watch. It can cost you some sleep, but it will provide the security you need when there's the slightest chance of your anchor dragging.

SITUATION 30:
Estimating Speed

You are heading for a small cove 62 miles away where you plan to spend the night. You and your crew departed at four in the morning since you want to arrive at your destination before nightfall.

Although your 26-foot sloop is not equipped with an electronic distance measuring device, you have streamed your patent log, which tells you distance run. You recently had it calibrated and are confident of its reliability.

It is 0800 now and as you assume the watch, you note distance run on the log's register. As you announce that you have already covered 18 miles and are averaging 4.5 knots, you see the log line go limp and stop rotating. About 30 meters aft you see the dorsal fin of a large gray fish. It is obvious that the shark has mistaken your log's rotator for a small fish and eaten it. You do not have a spare.

Although you continue to make good speed throughout the morning, the afternoon brings weaker winds and your boat slows. You have only a small outboard engine with enough fuel for in-port maneuvering.

How can you estimate your boat's speed?

HERE'S WHAT I'D DO . . .

SITUATION 30 Recommended Solution

Technology for measuring speed has improved greatly, but you'll have to use centuries-old techniques to calculate your boat speed. They're the same ones that Columbus relied on—improved just a little.

In his day, someone would throw an object overboard, a crew member would pace just fast enough to keep abreast of it as the boat passed by, and another person with a timepiece would record the elapsed time. If the pacer did not fall overboard and the timekeeper was accurate, the navigator could get a pretty good idea of speed.

Since then, the principles of calculating speed have not changed. They are expressed in the following formula:

$$\text{Speed} = \frac{\text{Distance}}{\text{Time}}$$

This formula is familiar to everyone. If, for example, you travel twenty miles in your automobile in half an hour, the arithmetic tells you your speed: 40 miles per hour (20/.5).

The situation you are faced with is more complicated because you do not know how far you have gone and you have no timekeeper aboard.

You can begin by using the length of your boat as distance, since you know it is 26 feet from stem to stern. Following Columbus' example, you could drop something overboard at the bow and let your boat pass it by.

The catch is the lack of a timepiece. But you'll surely have the materials aboard to fashion a rough clock. All it takes is a small weight such as a fishing sinker, and a piece of light line just 9.8 inches long (measured to the approximate center of gravity of the weight). Swung through any arc, your pendulum will complete one swing to and fro every second.

While your clock is "ticking," drop something light and buoyant overboard at the bow and count the number of seconds it takes it to clear your stern. If, for example, it took five seconds (meaning your boat travelled 26 feet in this amount of time), you can apply the basic formula that speed equals distance divided by time to figure out your speed. Properly expanded to reflect *knots* (6,080 feet per hour), the arithmetic looks like this:

$$\frac{26'}{5 \text{ sec.}} = \frac{312'}{1 \text{ min.}} = \frac{18,720'}{60 \text{ min.}} = \frac{3.1 \text{ nautical miles}}{1 \text{ hour}} = 3.1 \text{ knots}$$

Figure A provides the completed arithmetic for various boat lengths and elapsed times.

Approximate Speed in Knots Using Dutchman's Log

SECONDS	BOAT LENGTH				
	20'	*25'*	*30'*	*35'*	*40'*
1	11.8	14.7	17.8	20.8	23.6
2	5.9	7.4	8.9	10.4	11.8
3	3.9	4.9	5.9	6.9	7.9
4	3.0	3.7	4.5	5.2	5.9
5	2.4	2.9	3.6	4.2	4.7
6	2.0	2.4	3.0	3.5	3.9
7	1.7	2.1	2.5	3.0	3.4
8	1.5	1.8	2.2	2.6	2.9
9	1.3	1.6	2.0	2.3	2.6
10	1.2	1.5	1.8	2.1	2.4

Figure A

This technique, commonly known as a Dutchman's log, is great if you have plenty of crew and can station one forward (the dropper), one aft (the stern watcher), assign one as pendulum swinger, and be left with a helmsman. But it's certainly not workable for the often shorthanded cruising sailor, who will find it difficult to remain graceful and in control while rushing from bow to stern swinging a pendulum.

Probably the best method for you to use is the ancient chip-log technique, adjusted somewhat for the realities of the cruising sailor. In the old days, the sailor paid out a long line with a chip of wood at the end and a knot every 50 feet. He counted the number of knots which passed through his hand in 30 seconds' time, and estimated his speed. This, of course, is the origin of the word "knot" as a measure of both speed and distance.

On your small boat, you can use this technique with just one 51-foot line. In this case, you'll treat distance as a constant and time as the variable. Attach a piece of wood at the end of the line and use a free-spinning fishing reel to pay it out. Count the number of seconds it takes for the full 51 feet to stream behind your boat. Then divide the number of seconds into 30 to get your boat speed in knots.

For example, if it took six seconds for the 51-foot line to pay out, your boat's speed would be 30/6 or 5 knots.

For sailors who are opposed to all forms of arithmetic, Figure B shows various speed and time interval combinations.

Speed Over 51 Feet

TIME TO PAY OUT 51-FT. LINE	APPROXIMATE SPEED
30 seconds	1 knot
25 seconds	1.2 knots
20 seconds	1.5 knots
15 seconds	2.0 knots
10 seconds	3.0 knots
7.5 seconds	4.0 knots
6 seconds	5.0 knots
4.3 seconds	7.0 knots
3.8 seconds	8.0 knots
3.3 seconds	9.0 knots
3.0 seconds	10.0 knots

Figure B

RDF Bearings

Yesterday morning you left your home port and are sailing to a small island off the coast. The crossing is 165 nautical miles and you have only one landfall before getting to your destination.

You will rely on dead reckoning, your patent log, and your radio direction finder (RDF) for navigating. You do not have a sextant and there will be no opportunity for visual fixes along the way other than the landfall near your destination.

Your RDF receiver is a compact unit designed for small boats like yours. The small compass is mounted on top and, using the headphones provided, you simply rotate the unit until you find the "null," then note the beacon's bearing on the compass card.

You have consulted the list of radio and aeronautical beacons for the area. There are a number of stations along your route with sufficient range.

At 5 P.M. you take bearings on two marine radio beacons and one aeronautical radio beacon. You are confounded when you discover that the resulting lines of position place you 30 miles inland. You take the three bearings again with no improvement in accuracy.

What can you do to improve the quality of your RDF bearings?

HERE'S WHAT I'D DO . . .

So many things can go wrong with a position based solely on distant radio beacons that few cruising sailors would call it a "fix." At best, it is a rough estimate of your position. That is why your RDF set is called an "aid" to navigation, and why sailors try always to rely primarily on other methods such as soundings, celestial navigation, and bearings on sighted objects.

There are some things you can do to reduce the size of that cocked hat embarrassingly crisscrossing your chart. At least, if you recognize some of the limitations of RDF (and they are substantial), you'll be able to guard against them and minimize their effect on your navigation.

What you're listening for, of course, is the "null" from the station you've selected. By rotating the antenna loop to a point where its plane is toward the beacon, you get a strong, clear signal. When you continue rotating it another 90 degrees, the plane of the loop is perpendicular to the beacon, and the signal power is zero—the "null" that serves as an indication of bearing.

Since the null occurs twice while you rotate the antenna through 360 degrees, it can be ambiguous—180 degrees off. Some RDF sets have sense indicators which resolve this ambiguity, but yours does not. Consequently, you will have to guard against drawing lines of position which are reciprocals of the actual LOPs. Applying common sense usually works in this case, yet seven U.S. destroyers were lost in 1923 when an RDF operator failed to distinguish between true and reciprocal bearings off Point Concepcion in California.

Another technique to prevent ambiguities is to plot at least two RDF bearings. The intersections resulting effectively resolve these uncertainties.

Even under the best of circumstances, the null area for a radio beacon is at least 2 degrees wide. Although this is not a problem for beacons which are less than 50 miles distant, the resulting cone for bearings at greater distances can be very large. If, for example, you plot two bearings from radio beacons both 100 miles distant, the resulting "fix" is an area covering more than 30 square miles!

Of course you can't do anything about this built-in error except recognize that it exists. But you can reduce other kinds of error that affect your calculations.

Deviation is one of them. Just as your steering compass is affected by masses of metal on your boat, RDFs have their form of deviation. It is called "quadrantal error," since its effect is greatest at relative angles of 45° and 135° on both sides of the boat. Although it should not have much effect on a fiberglass boat, it can raise havoc on a steel hull. You can check for quadrantal error next time you are within visual range of an RDF beacon. Make check bearings while turning your boat through 360°. It is possible that the rigging or life rails on your boat is causing the problem. Be sure to stand as far away from them and the mast as possible while you are taking bearings.

The earphones can also be a source of significant error. If, like most navigators, you sit comfortably in the main cabin hunched over the hand-held receiver, the magnetic sound unit at the "V" in the earphones could be as little as two inches away from the compass. This is one of the most common causes of error. There should be at least one foot separating the sound pressure unit and the compass, making for awkward posture but more accurate bearings.

You've probably noticed how much better radio reception seems to be at night, particularly at dawn and dusk. This is caused by movements of the reflective ionosphere layer of the atmosphere. While great for entertainment radio, this bouncing of waves plays havoc with radio beacon waves. You can reduce this effect by doing the obvious —limiting nighttime RDF bearings—and being sure the stations you select are within the ranges shown in the radio lists.

If any of the bearings you've taken come from signals which must travel over land—especially at an oblique angle up or down a coast— the errors you're getting may be caused by a phenomenon called coastal refraction. The radio waves actually bend back toward the coast, yielding a false bearing.

Always try to take three bearings, preferably about 120° from each other. You'll always get a cocked hat, but if it's small enough, you can take the center of the triangle as your estimated position.

Although RDFs have some real limitations, they are without equal as homing devices. But like all electronic aids, some common sense needs to be used in their operation. The Nantucket light ship was sunk by a ship homing on it.

When homing, remember that you never know how far away from the transmitter you are, unless you take some cross-bearings or use your depth sounder. It is always a good idea to steer off a bit from your homing course in order to reduce the possibility of collision.

SITUATION 32:
Collision

You're in one of the world's busiest shipping lanes, about to enter the traffic separation zones. The assembly of freighters, ferry boats, coasters, and supertankers is awesome.

The weather is fine, though, and you expect to make port before nightfall. The 12-knot breeze out of the west should continue throughout the day, providing you with a pleasant ride in your 26-foot sloop.

You notice a large tanker off your port bow. It is heading in your direction. You figure it's about four miles distant.

Although the tanker is going to pass in your general area, you believe it will present no problem.

Settling back, you enjoy the pleasant sail. Approximately six minutes have passed since you first noticed the tanker.

You're shocked when you next look to port. The tanker is blocking out most of your view! She is so close, in fact, that you can see the officer of the watch on the wing of the bridge.

The concept of a collision course jolts you out of your shock. What should you do? What should you have done when you first noticed the tanker?

What are the basic rules of the road of which the cruising sailor must be aware?

HERE'S WHAT I'D DO . . .

SITUATION 32 *Recommended Solution*

First, assume that the tanker is doing, at minimum, 20 knots. A quick calculation using the basic formula of "Distance = Rate × Time" should tell you that she is covering four miles every 12 minutes! In six minutes the tanker has exactly *halved* the distance to your boat.

Second, notice that the bearing angle between you and the tanker has not changed. This constant bearing spells danger to you, since the fact that it is not changing makes it a *collision* bearing. If you do not change course, she'll hit you. Why is it necessary for *you* to make the course alteration? After all, you think, "I'm under sail, she's under power. I have the right-of-way." At this point, it may be impossible for the tanker captain to materially affect the course or speed of his ship. It could take three to five miles for him to bring the tanker to a full stop, and her responses to changes in rudder angle are at best sluggish.

The cruising sailor must, in congested waters, sail as drivers are taught to drive: defensively. *You* will have to make a course change, fast, probably coming about away from the tanker, and reversing your course. It would also be a good idea to get your engine started as quickly as possible to give you maximum speed away from this danger. (Be sure to look aft before you turn around—there may be another behemoth bearing down on you from behind. Indeed, this may explain why the tanker cannot change course!)

Sure, the new International Rules for Preventing Collisions do give you priority over the tanker (except in narrow channels), but you mustn't rely on this. The tanker crew simply may not see you, their radar system may "lose" you in the seaway or may not be operating, or there may be no one on the bridge. Too many "ifs"—the cruising sailor is a fool to demand right-of-way in this situation. The best thing to assume is that you have *not* been seen.

Even if the tanker's radar system is working perfectly, you don't really know how good your radar "signature" is. Current radar systems are pretty unlikely to discriminate between your boat and the heavy sea clutter common in medium to high seas. Be sure your octahedral reflector is hung at least five meters high to deal with waves and swell.

Remember these basic collision avoidance rules:

1. Between large ships under power and your sailboat, your right-of-way means little. Do not demand it. Sail defensively. Maintain course and speed only if it is obvious that the powered ship is giving way to you.

2. Between you and another sailboat, you can be more demanding. Starboard tack has right-of-way over port, and the leeward boat has right-of-way over the windward, if you're both on the same tack.

3. If you're under power and meet up with another boat under power in a crossing situation, the boat to starboard has the right-of-way. A handy mnemonic device for remembering this is to think of your starboard running light (green) as a "go" signal for the boat off your starboard bow.

4. If you're overtaking another vessel, you must keep clear of it. It has the right-of-way.

SITUATION 33:
Medical Emergencies

Before leaving on a three-day cruise, you and your wife stop at a small village downriver to purchase supplies. When the tiny quay comes into view, you discover that there is no room alongside. You turn your twenty-eight foot sloop into the current and approach the smallest raft of six boats.

After asking permission to come alongside, you secure to a small fiberglass catamaran. After making bow and stern lines fast, you ask your wife to take a bow line ashore. You pay out ten fathoms of line as she crosses from bow to bow, taking the line around each forestay. Once on the quay, she secures it with a bowline to a bollard.

Returning to your boat, she places her full weight on the corner of a closed hatch on the catamaran. It tilts open and your wife screams as her right leg crashes into the inboard engine space. She clambers back aboard wincing in pain. You notice a lot of blood where the engine cut into her leg and have her lie down in the main cabin. While cleansing the wound you are relieved to see that she does not have a compound fracture, but you can detect a broken bone. Her right shin is beginning to swell.

There are no doctors or medical services immediately available, but you believe you can get your wife to an emergency room in six hours or so.

What kind of first aid do you administer now?

HERE'S WHAT I'D DO . . .

SITUATION 33 Recommended Solution

Medical emergencies aboard cruising sailboats occur, unfortunately, with great frequency. Most of them are of the stubbed toe variety, necessitating nothing more than a little tender loving care and a bit of first aid knowledge. Some however, are more traumatic, nasty things like cardiac arrest, burns, and near-drowning. Most male skippers seem to delegate responsibility for the medical side of things to the female on board, somehow believing that she will never need first aid herself. This is a shortsighted and dangerous attitude. Knowledge of basic first aid is something that everyone needs to master!

A simple leg fracture falls somewhere in the mid-range of shipboard crises, requiring thoughtful, well-informed first aid attention. You can do more harm than good in this situation. For example, one of the problems a layman faces in helping a person with a simple fracture is compounding it by pushing the bone ends through the skin.

The first thing to do to help your wife is to remain calm. Fake it if you must, but do not let your internal panic affect her. Don't rush. You have plenty of time to take things slowly.

Think what you have to deal with in this medical emergency. First, there is the bleeding. You'll want to stop that in fairly quick order. Next, turn your attention to the fracture itself. Fortunately, it's a simple one with no bone protruding through the skin. Finally, be sensitive to the risk of shock; if untreated, this could be very serious.

To deal with the bleeding, do what doctors do: use simple pressure at the site of the wound. If, after three to five minutes, the pressure you've applied with a sterile gauze pad hasn't stemmed the flow, try again. If blood soaks through the pad, but doesn't clot, don't change the pad. Add others and continue the pressure. If blood still flows, try to determine where it's coming from. Arterial blood flows in spurts; venous blood is steady. Use a tourniquet as a last resort *only* in the case of spurting arterial blood. Be sure to loosen it frequently to prevent damage to blood vessels and nerves.

Once the bleeding has stopped, meticulously wash your hands and clean the wound carefully. If it is a relatively small surface wound, you can close it with sterile gauze and adhesive tape. A large and/or deep wound may require stitches to close it. Don't hesitate to use your sail repair kit and a pair of pliers (all scrubbed and then soaked in alcohol) as a suture kit.

At all times, keep a wary eye out for signs of shock. The symptoms are any or all of the following: nausea, vomiting, pale clammy skin, rapid weak pulse, faintness. Shock can kill; if you detect any of these signs, *immediately* take these steps:

- Keep the victim calm and quiet
- Keep the victim warm and dry
- Elevate the victim's legs

Contrary to popular belief, a shot of alcohol will not help the victim, and may do harm. If you are certain there are no internal injuries, and if the patient is conscious and not vomiting, a warm beverage can be given.

Your wife's leg must be immobilized until you can get her to expert medical help. Use your creativity to come up with some sort of splint. This is no problem on a sailboat. One of your dinghy oars (shortened down quickly with a saw, of course), a boat hook, mop or broom handle, bottom board, or even that pile of yachting magazines you've been saving will do. The splint must project beyond the surrounding joints in order to do its job, so make it long enough to reach from her ankle to above the knee. Pad it well with rags, cotton, or what-have-you for a good, form-fitting contour. Tie it on with line or torn-up sheets, and be sure it's not too tight. Otherwise, it could interfere with the flow of blood. If her foot feels cold or numb or begins to discolor, loosen the splint. Keep the leg elevated to reduce swelling.

Finally, get your wife to professional help as quickly as possible.

Although no one looks forward to shipboard medical emergencies, the essence of rewarding cruising is a fair amount of self-reliance. Being able to stand in capably until the experts can be summoned is as important for sailors as knowing the difference between the leech and the luff.

If you don't have a good, up-to-date first aid manual on board, get one and read it. It's as valuable an asset as your boat insurance!

SITUATION 34:
Sailing the Anchor Out

You have spent the day in a beautiful, but exposed, anchorage down the coast. Yours is the only boat in the crescent-shaped bay. Before nightfall, you don snorkel and fins in order to check the anchor. It is well set in the sand and mud bottom.

Just after sunrise the next morning, you are awakened by the noise of wind in the rigging of your 30-foot sloop. On checking, you discover that a 180° shift in the wind has put you off a lee shore. Although you are not dragging, you know you must depart as soon as possible.

After waking your guests, you ventilate the engine space and push the starter button. The low, grinding moan you hear is the unmistakable complaint of a near-dead battery. The motor has no hand crank. Your new power anchor windlass is useless, since its hydraulics depend on the main engine and it has no back-up hand power arrangement. When one of your crew tries to haul on the chain, the increasing wind makes it impossible. You realize you'll have to weigh anchor under sail.

What's your plan?

HERE'S WHAT I'D DO . . .

SITUATION 34 *Recommended Solution*

Weighing anchor under sail is not the easiest thing in the world to do, but it most assuredly can be done. Thousands of sailing craft without engines do it every day; for many years, it was the only way to go. If they can do it, you can do it!

Take some time to think out what your plan will be. Be sure that your crew members are aware of what you want and how you want them to do it.

You'll want at least one of them—preferably the biggest and burliest of the bunch—at the bow tending the anchor chain. This person must be told that his fingers are in real jeopardy if he's not careful. Give him a good heavy pair of leather gloves for additional protection.

If your boat sails handily under main alone (many do), hoist it. Get the jib hanked on, complete with halyard at the ready just in case, but keep it in ties. You won't want to use it unless it's necessary for tacking, since it will get in the way of your bow crew's work. If you're not confident of your boat's ability to go to weather under main alone, be sure to hoist the foresail.

Fortunately, there are no other boats in the area and you have plenty of room to maneuver. Either tack will be acceptable for getting under way.

There are at least two ways to get started. Both have their advantages, and you'll need to decide which one to use, depending on the situation. You can have the bow crew quickly pay out additional rode, allowing you to make sternway while positioning the rudder to put the bows down. Or, you can swing the main out on a preventer, which will provide the torque necessary to get the bows off the wind. If the jib is up, backing it with a sheet to windward will help accomplish the same objective.

Once under way, coordination between you and the crew at the bow becomes critical. When you start moving, be sure that all the slack in the anchor chain is hauled in. As soon as it comes taut, have the bow crew quickly take a turn around the samson post, being sure not to get fingers in between it and the rode. There must be a pre-arranged signal to tell you when the chain is secured.

On this signal, put the helm over and come about. If you're extremely lucky, this first tack will put you over the anchor and it will lift out smartly when the bow crew next takes a turn around the samson post. More than likely, however, you'll be forced to do several tacks before it breaks out.

The rode, even though slack, will offer a lot of resistance and may tend to pull the bows into the wind, making it impossible to sail. If this occurs, move it aft, closer to the pivot point of your boat. Although this requires some almost superhuman footwork as you come about, it may be necessary on the first couple of tacks.

If you are really unlucky and there is a current causing the wind to be abaft your beam as you lay to your anchor, you should not use the main. It will be unmanageable with the wind behind it. You may, however, use the foresail to run down to the anchor slowly, spilling air out of it to maintain control.

If all else fails, you should not hesitate to abandon the anchor and its rode. If you've buoyed it with a trip line or simply tied a fender onto the end of the rode, it will be easily retrieved when you return in more settled weather. With chain, abandonment will no doubt mean a quick trip to the chain locker with knife in hand to release the bitter end of the rode.

SITUATION 35:
Diagnosing Engine Troubles

You've just completed a fine day of sailing, with three guests aboard, when the wind goes flat and dies. In the heavy swell, the sails slat wildly back and forth. After waiting a few minutes, you decide to motor the rest of the way. After getting the sails handed, you "sniff test" the engine space. Thus assured that there is no fuel leak, you turn the key and press the starter button.

The gasoline powered engine turns over, but will not start. You repeatedly attempt to start it, but this only seems to result in flooding the carburetor and draining the strength of your battery.

What steps do you take to diagnose the problem and get the engine started?

HERE'S WHAT I'D DO . . .

SITUATION 35 Recommended Solution

Although you may not be able to do major engine overhauls, you can easily carry out some basic diagnostic work to determine the cause of your engine problem.

Your boat's engine consists of four interrelated systems: fuel, ignition, cooling, and electrical. The cooling system wouldn't cause starting problems, and the starter motor wouldn't even turn over if the generator hadn't charged up the battery. Start with the most obvious possibility. Check the fuel system. It may seem unbelievable, but a vast majority of failures to start the engine are caused by lack of fuel— either the tank is empty or a valve leading from the tank to the fuel filter or carburetor has not been opened.

Once you are sure you are not out of gas, check to see if gasoline is getting to the carburetor. The vibrations set up aboard a boat have a nasty way of working the most secure fuel lines loose, or breaking them altogether. Your nose should provide you with an instant warning of a gas leak, but a visual inspection is also called for. If you should discover a leak, with gasoline ending up in the bilge, treat your boat for what it is, a floating bomb! Until those heavier-than-air fumes have been vented from the hull, real caution is necessary. Use a hand bilge pump to remove the gasoline, not an electric one which could cause a spark.

If there is no leak, remove a spark plug to see if gasoline is getting through the carburetor to the cylinders. They should be moist with gasoline and have the telltale smell. If they're dripping wet, the system is still flooded from your attempts to get the motor started earlier. Go back to ground zero and try starting again after waiting five minutes or so. (Have the choke and throttle open.)

If the engine keeps flooding, the smell of gasoline will probably be overpowering. No doubt your problem is centered in the float bowl of your carburetor. This device is designed to meter the amount of gasoline being mixed with air to form the explosive vapor that makes it all happen. When the bowl fills, the float rises, forcing a narrow valve into a seat. If a particle of something or other has gotten into the works, the float may not rise properly and the valve may not close. Result: flooding. Treatment: bash away on the outside of the float bowl with something not too massive, like the handle of a screwdriver. This may well free the system. If not, you'll have to dismantle the float chamber and clean it.

If the plugs are dry, you've found the problem: its name is "fuel system obstruction." If your carburetor has been flooding, the problem is probably between the carburetor and the cylinders. If not, it's between the tank and the carburetor, requiring that you remove the lines, blow them clean, and clean the fuel filter as well. It's important that there be a shut-off valve at the tank to prevent leakage while you dismantle the plumbing.

If the plugs are moist, you can, for the moment, assume that the fuel system is in good working order. (Don't get too confident, though, since the fuel could be dirty or full of water.) Since the explosive vapor being sucked into the cylinders needs a source of ignition, the next place to check is the ignition system.

The spark plugs simply won't spark if there's a foul-up in the ignition system. Diagnosis starts with finding out whether or not a robust amount of voltage is being delivered to them. Remove one of the plug wires and insert a small screwdriver into the connector device. While turning the engine over, hold the shaft of the screwdriver about a quarter-inch away from an unpainted part of the engine. If you can get a spark to leap across, you know that juice is going to the plugs.

No doubt the reason your engine won't start is fouled spark plugs, one of the commonest maladies plaguing cruising sailboats. Remove each plug and see whether or not it is oily and/or covered with a brownish crusty deposit. Clean it up or replace it with a new one. Chances are good that this will solve your problem. An easy way to check for misfiring plugs, if you can get the engine going, is to put it in idle and remove the plug wires one at a time. The faulty plug will *not* cause a decrease in engine speed.

If there is no spark when you do the screwdriver test, your problem is probably in the distributor or the coil. You'll hope that it is the distributor, since it can be repaired under way. The coil usually cannot.

Take off the distributor cap and check for moisture and cracks. Pull off the rotor and make sure its contacts are clean. Also check the contacts in the cap to be sure they are clean. Finally, observe the contact points as the engine is turned over. They should be free of carbon and you will just be able to make out a spark as they open and close. A weak spark, or none at all, is indicative of coil or condenser problems.

Chances are very good that you've located and been able to fix the problem using the above information. If the engine still won't start, there's one last thing to check. Did you by any chance lose a line over the side while you were handing the sails? It could be fouled in your propeller. This will bind up even the most powerful auxiliary engine. A quick dive below, knife in hand, should get that mess untangled.

SITUATION 36:
Docking Under Sail

Although the engine in your 33-foot sloop is inoperative due to trans-mission problems, the afternoon breeze is too good to pass up. You decide to get under way for a short sail.

Your departure is perfect, the offshore wind pushing you gently away from the head of the pontoon while you hoist main and jib.

In the late afternoon, as you are returning to the marina with a fair Force 5 wind behind you, you become a bit apprehensive. Docking a heavy displacement, long keel cruiser without the aid of an engine is bound to be difficult.

What's your strategy for getting alongside under sail power?

HERE'S WHAT I'D DO . . .

SITUATION 36 *Recommended Solution*

Anyone can learn to bring a boat up to a mooring or alongside a dock under power. Getting a heavy-displacement cruiser alongside a dock under sail power alone—without damaging topsides and self-respect —is a certifiable act of real seamanship.

If you've had any practice at all in the fine art of shooting moorings or man-overboard retrieval under sail, you'll have a halfway decent understanding of how your sloop carries into the wind, handles under jib alone, and how long she takes to come about. This knowledge will serve you well now, as you face the challange of maneuvering in close quarters.

Start by promising yourself that you won't yield to the temptation to rush things. You'll make a few turns around the dockside before deciding on your final approach strategy, gauging conditions. This is a good time to get the anchor out of its chocks and ready for use. The essence of good seamanship is knowing when to quit the fancy stuff and "hang it up" before making a real mess out of things.

As soon as the dock comes into view, decide on the spot you wish to take. Ideally, there should be plenty of space fore and aft so that you'll come out smelling like a rose if you misjudge anything.

Your choice of position alongside will be controlled by two things: space available and wind direction (assuming there is no current running). Hope you'll be able to find a place where your final maneuver will be dead into the wind. If not, your task becomes considerably more complicated.

If the wind is blowing parallel to the dockside, for example, you can close reach up to a position a few feet off, head into the wind, sails luffing, and get lines over. Most boats will handle quite adequately under one sail, so you may want to get the jib hauled down to minimize the confusion its luffing will cause forward.

Downwind approach? Well, one rule deals with this. Never, never, approach a large immobile object like a dock downwind unless there is no alternative.

When the wind is blowing hard with strong seas behind you, it's next to impossible to control the situation. If you feel you have no alternative, however, the approach should be made in the following way: While still a good ways off the dock, round up and get the main down. It will become unmanageable on a downwind run when you must stop before colliding with the wood and cement ahead. Then, bear off with jib alone. As soon as it appears you can make it the rest of the way, hand the jib or let it run free downwind. Be sure to have a large supply of fenders ready to protect your topsides from the bashing they could get as soon as you arrive alongside.

If the dock is downwind and conditions are at all rough, the best approach is to round up a considerable distance off the dock, drop anchor (using your best crew), and pay out the rode, backing your sloop down to the dock where sternlines can be secured.

If the wind is blowing away from the dock (perpendicular), the approach is straightforward. Be sure and get the main handed and use the foresail by itself. The after shrouds will prevent the main from spilling all the wind, and it will keep driving the boat forward, making it difficult to stop where you want to. The jib sheet, though, can be slackened at the right moment, causing the sail to lose almost all of its drive.

One thing is critical about docking under sail. When you come alongside, you must be going dead slow. Anything over a half-knot is unacceptable and will quickly provide a dramatic example of what happens when you try to stop 12 tons of kinetic energy with a quick jerk. Although some sailors recommend heroic slowing maneuvers like backing the main (imagine the strength this would require in a good breeze), swinging the rudder to and fro (guaranteed to make dockside observers think you've gone crazy), or easing out a midships spring line around a jib winch, the only real solution is to sail the boat to a stop in the right place. Then, get lines over for a little fine-tuning of an otherwise perfect landing.

Bobbing a Light

You're returning from a week-long cruise in the Gulf of Maine in your 26-foot sloop. The weather has been excellent, and you have decided to continue sailing throughout the night.

As this was your idea, you've been awarded the mid-watch. There is no moon and the visibility is excellent. You are thoroughly awed by the beauty of nighttime sailing and are pleased with your ability to identify many of the stars and planets used for navigation.

When you checked the Light List yesterday, you found that Halfway Rock Light should be visible sometime before dawn, assuming of course that you were able to maintain your average speed of four knots.

At three thirty in the morning, you go forward to set the whisker pole. You see a red-flashing light just on the horizon. The flashing continues for just three seconds, then stops. As this matches the characteristics for Halfway Rock Light, you're pretty sure you know where you are. Returning to the cockpit, you pull out your stopwatch and wait for the red flashes, which should occur every 90 seconds, to reappear.

They do not. Even when you use your binoculars, the red flashes are not visible. Only when you return to the foredeck can you make out the light off your starboard bow.

Once you've determined the true bearing of Halfway Rock using your hand-held compass, you wonder how far away it is.

How can you calculate your distance from the lighthouse, assuming it is the only visible aid to navigation available?

HERE'S WHAT I'D DO . . .

SITUATION 37 Recommended Solution

Although you cannot get a definite fix from observations made on Halfway Rock Light, you can get a good estimate of your position. First, the bearing you've taken gives you a line of position. If you can estimate your distance from the light, an arc can be scribed across the LOP, yielding an estimated position.

Whenever a light disappears and then reappears as you move from cockpit to deck or up the mast, you have a unique opportunity to calculate its distance from your position. This is called "bobbing" a light.

This chance to estimate your position, occurring only when each light comes into view at the horizon, explains why cruising sailors expend so much energy trying to spot the first flash of light.

The distance a light may be seen depends on several things—the candlepower of the light, atmospheric conditions, the height of the observer's eye above sea level, and the height of the light itself above the sea. Each must be taken into consideration when you determine your distance from a light on the horizon. The "nominal range" of all major lights is published in the Light List. This is the distance at which a light can be seen in clear weather, and is a function of candlepower and color of the light. Colors make a big difference in visibility; short wavelengths are less powerful than longer wavelengths.

If you're wondering what the authors of the Light List mean when they say "clear weather," it's defined as visibility of ten nautical miles. Anyone who has searched the sky for navigational lights in fog or haze knows how much atmospheric conditions can affect visibility. Things like dust particles and water droplets in the air tend to weaken a beam of light by scattering and diffusing its rays.

When you changed your position in the boat from the deck level to the cockpit and back, you were able to "bob" the light—to make it appear and disappear on the horizon. This is possible because you and

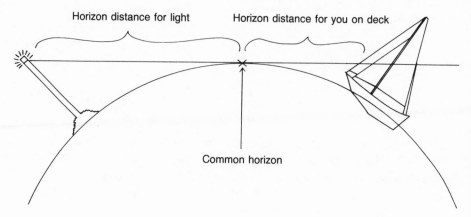

Horizon distance for light   Horizon distance for you on deck

Common horizon

Figure A

the light "share" the same horizon, as shown in Figure A. When you lowered your height of eye as you reentered the cockpit, the flashing red light was no longer visible. It was, in fact, "over" your horizon.

Horizon distance is a function of height and can easily be calculated by the following formula:

$$\text{Horizon Distance In Nautical Miles} = 1.14 \; \sqrt{\text{Height}}$$

Normal refraction of light rays is taken into consideration in the formula.

The nominal ranges shown in the Light Lists assume that your height of eye is 15 feet above sea level. No doubt that is why they are called "nominal," as this is seldom the case. Consequently, you'll have to know your height of eye when standing on deck or sitting in the cockpit.

But the Light List will give you a perfectly adequate height above sea level for the light. With this you can calculate its horizon distance. Adding the two together (your horizon distance plus that of the light) gives you an estimate of your distance from the light.

For example, if your height of eye above sea level is nine feet, your horizon distance is 3.4 nautical miles ($1.14 \times \sqrt{9}$). The Light List tells you that Halfway Rock Light is 76 feet above the water. Its horizon distance is, therefore, 9.9 nautical miles ($1.14 \times \sqrt{76}$).

When you add the two horizon distances together, you have an estimate of the distance between you and the light: $9.9 + 3.4 = 13.3$ nautical miles.

Now you can scribe an arc representing this distance across your bearing line for Halfway Rock Lighthouse. This will provide you with an estimated position. Remember, though, that due to the vagaries of atmospheric conditions, refraction of light waves, and so forth, it is not accurate enough to be labelled a fix.

Beware of lights on the horizon which seem to flash on and off at odd moments. Even the most astute observer won't be able to see a discernable pattern. These mysterious signals are probably coming from fishing boats or other small craft using bright lights. As they bob up and down in a seaway, they often appear, at first glance, to be aids to navigation. This they definitely are not.

Estimating Distance-Off

You're two-and-a-half days out of port, heading for a large island several hundred miles off the coast. The barometer is falling and you know a storm is brewing.

Your plan is to head for the closest well-protected harbor. You're picking up a strong RDF signal from the transmitter near the port, but there is no other signal with which to triangulate your position. You are not confident about your dead-reckoning fix.

On approximately the same bearing as the RDF transmitter, the top of a mountain peak is just visible on the horizon at great distance. Your chart shows this peak to be 1,485 meters (4,900 feet) above sea level.

Since you want to enter the harbor only during daylight to avoid off-lying dangers, you'd like to know how many miles you have left to go.

Can you calculate how far you are from port?

HERE'S WHAT I'D DO . . .

You *can* figure out how far away port is. Doing it, however, requires that you know the easy formula for something called "horizon distance." This is the distance from you (or anything else, for that matter) to the horizon.

We'll get to the formula in a moment. First, think about the problem for a minute. You've got a good RDF bearing but nothing to triangulate your position from, since the mountain peak is almost directly behind the cape. But, if you can figure out how far you are from the mountain, you could draw a distance circle on the chart, providing you with a fix.

There's only one criterion which must be met to use this technique: you and the object you're sighting must "share" the same horizon. The best way to explain this is the drawing in Figure A.

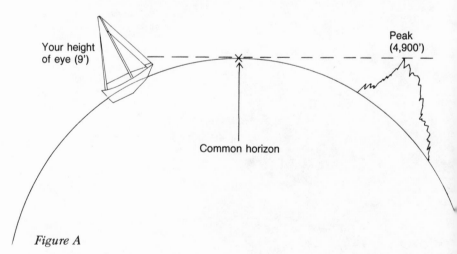

Figure A

If, and *only* if, this requirement is met, you can use this technique. It's simple, requiring only that you calculate the distance between you and the horizon and the distance between the mountain peak and the same horizon.

Start by calculating the distance between you and the horizon. This is done using the formula:

Distance in miles $= 1.15 \times \sqrt{H}$, where "H" is the height (in feet) of your eye above sea level.

Having measured this before, you know that your height of eye when standing in your cockpit is nine feet. Since the square root of 9 is 3, the horizon must be 3.45 miles away.

Now you must add the distance the mountain peak is away—on the "other side" of the horizon. It's charted at 1,485 meters above sea level, or about 4,900 feet. Using the same formula for horizon distance, you calculate that the peak is about 80.5 miles from the horizon:

Distance in miles $= 1.15 \times \sqrt{4,900} = 1.15 \times 70 = 80.5$

Now, adding this distance to the distance you are away from the horizon (3.45 miles), you figure you're about 84 miles away from the mountain.

Next step: scribe the distance circle on your chart, intersecting the RDF bearing line. This fix shows your distance from port and protection if the storm should happen to kick up.

Incidentally, if calculating square roots isn't your cup of tea, don't immediately decide to buy an electronic calculator. Handy and inexpensive as they are, most aren't designed for use in a salt water environment. Their unreliability aboard sailboats is notorious. The solution is the modern-day dinosaur known as a slide rule. A slide rule may be hard to come by in this age of silicon chips and semiconductors, but they're absolutely super for chores like calculating square roots. And, they don't need batteries.

SITUATION 39:
Interpreting Chart Symbols

After a week of sailing coastwise from Newport Beach to San Francisco, the Golden Gate finally comes into view about six miles off your starboard bow. Adjusting course to the east, you are able to run with twin headsails set.

After settling down on a comfortable run, you review your charts for entrance to the bay. Completing a fix on One Mile Rock and the north end of the Golden Gate Bridge, you notice the following symbol on the chart in front of your position:

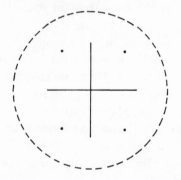

Quickly checking Chart No. 1, you conclude that this symbol means "rocks awash" and proceed on, carefully searching the horizon in front of you for a small rock or islet.

The wind soon dies out completely. You hand the sails and enter the main cabin to turn on the battery switch before starting the engine. Just as you step back into the cockpit, you're thrown onto the cabin sole. Your boat has hit that rock.

What critical mistake in chart reading did you make?

HERE'S WHAT I'D DO . . .

SITUATION 39 *Recommended Solution*

Sailing charts are crammed with so much information that much of it must be shown in shortened form. Symbols and abbreviations are used in almost all cases. The definitions of these symbols and abbreviations are given in the Defense Mapping Agency's Chart No. 1. There are so many definitions required that this "chart" is in actuality a 25-page booklet.

Although it would be extremely difficult to commit all of these to memory, some are so important that you mustn't rely on a quick reference to Chart No. 1 for details while you are involved in conning your boat. The symbol for "rock awash" is certainly a critical one.

The most important symbols are those which identify dangers. There are 49 of these listed in the "Danger" section of Chart No. 1. Many of them are quite easy to commit to memory after a quick inspection, since the graphics are stylized representations of the real thing. Figure A gives two good examples.

But what about that symbol you saw on the chart in front of your fix? Sure, a quick reference to Chart No. 1 mentions "rock awash," but it *also* tells you that the dotted circle surrounding the symbol means "danger to navigation."

If you had been thoroughly familiar with the important danger section of Chart No. 1, you would have realized that the rock might not have been visible at the surface of the water and adjusted course to avoid the area.

The difficulties in interpreting chart symbols become greater if you are using two charts from different sources, such as the U.S. Defense Mapping Agency and the British Admiralty. Although international conferences have been held to attempt standardization, these committees have been unable to reach agreement. Consequently, in the case of the excellent British Admiralty charts, you'll need Admiralty Chart No. 5011 for interpretation of the symbols and abbreviations.

In addition to memorizing all the symbols for dangers, the way the

Symbol	Meaning

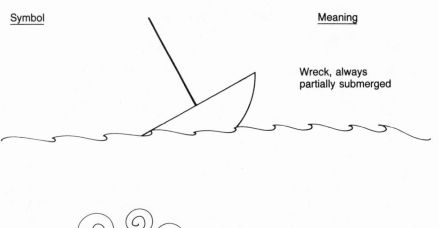

Wreck, always partially submerged

Eddies

Figure A

type is printed can help you know when you are standing into danger. Vertical type is used exclusively for those land elements on the chart which are dry at high water, the visibility of which is unaffected by movement of the water. Italicized lettering is reserved for water elements which are either at the water line, underwater, or floating.

Sometimes, as you switch from small scale charts (used for passages) to large scale charts (used for close-in maneuvering at the coast or in harbor), you'll find that the technique for indicating depth differs.

Although the British Admiralty charts are being changed, many still show depth in fathoms (six feet), while the newer ones show depth in meters. Many U.S. charts show depth in feet. Some charts show depth only by fathom lines. These dots and dashes are simple to interpret once you know the "key" (see Figure B).

Finally, charts which show depths in figures representing fathoms become a bit confusing for many cruising sailors in areas where the

Depth Contour Lines

FATHOMS	LEGEND
3	· · · · · · · · · · · · · · · · · · · · ·
4	· · · · · · · · · · · · · · · · · · · · · · · ·
5	· · · · · · · · · · · · · · · · · · · · · · · · ·
10	— · — · — · — · — · — · — · — · — · — · — ·
20	· · — · · — · · — · · — · · — · · — · · — · · —
50	· · · · · — — — — — — · · · · · — — — — —

Figure B

depth is less than 11 fathoms. In these shoal waters, the depth figures may look like this:

$$7_6 \qquad 10_3$$
$$3_5$$

This is a combination legend for shallow waters. The first figure refers to fathoms, the subscript to feet.

SITUATION 40:

Interpreting Navigational Lights

This cruise will include your first overnight passage. You have wisely installed high-power bulbs in your side lights, and have invested in a new masthead light. You also are equipped with a 300,000 candle-power searchlight.

Since you are concerned about knowing what other ships are doing, you have carefully studied the Rules of the Road.

At ten thirty in the evening, you spot two white lights, one above the other. Although you cannot make out any other lights yet, you're certain it is a large ship under power coming toward you. A few minutes later you can make out both red and green side lights. You are amazed at the speed with which this ship, now clearly a very large one, is closing on you.

Since the lower of the two white lights is slightly to the left of the higher one, and you can make out a red running light, you believe the tanker is going to pass from your right to left. As you quickly jibe your boat around to avoid what now appears to be a close call, you reconfirm that the lower of the two white lights is to the left.

You can't believe your eyes when you see that the tanker is now turning to port, toward you. She is so close now that her running lights are hidden by her massive bows. You can clearly hear the rumbling of her engines as she bears down on you.

You jibe once again and scream to your crew to get the engine started. At full power, you're just able to get clear of the speeding tanker. You're so close that the wash from her propellers puts green water into your cockpit.

After things calm down a bit, you pull out the Rules of the Road. Just as you suspected, they call for large ships under power to carry two masthead lights, one at the bow and one aft. The after light is supposed to be at least 15 feet higher than the forward one.

What mistake did you make? What navigational lights must the cruising sailor be familiar with?

HERE'S WHAT I'D DO . . .

SITUATION 40 Recommended Solution

The two white lights which you were watching so closely are called "range lights." Their purpose is to help you figure out another boat's heading in relation to yours. At normal distances, they give the cruising sailor an early warning signal so that avoiding action can be taken if a ship is on a collision course.

However, the International Rules of the Road are primarily designed to prevent collisions between large ships, and sometimes do not consider the odd perspective from a small boat only a few feet above sea level.

In this case, the first view you had of the tanker's running lights rightly suggested that she would pass from your right to left, as the lower, forward light was to the left of the after masthead light. This is shown in Figure A.

Figure A

Crossing from right to left

However, as the tanker got very close to you, say a quarter of a mile or so, your angle of vision "up" to her bows changed the relative relationship of the two critical range lights, as shown in Figure B.

The authors of the Rules of the Road recognized the possibility of this optical illusion, and called for the lights on large ships to be separated so that the after light would be seen over the forward light when viewed from sea level. But this requirement is for a viewer at least one kilometer away. When the distance is less, it's possible for the lights

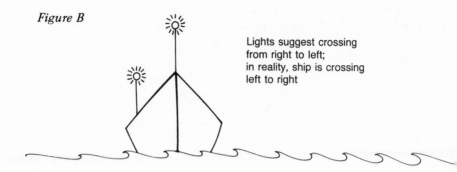

Figure B

Lights suggest crossing
from right to left;
in reality, ship is crossing
left to right

to appear to reverse themselves, leading to errors in concluding which way the large vessel is heading.

Fortunately, this kind of misinterpretation of navigational lights is rare. Although international conferences held during the past years have consistently failed to come up with a worldwide system of light rules (U.S. sailors are faced with no less than four different systems), the resulting confusion can be reduced to some easily understood basics.

First, the cruising sailor should realize that there are just six major types of running lights for all boats and ships (excluding the hand-held flashlight required by boats under oars). Of these, two are rarely seen —the towing light and the flashing light. These six lights and their characteristics are shown in Figure C.

Once you've learned the vocabulary, you can start interpreting what various combinations mean.

Most tables which show lights for various types of vessels are as complicated and difficult to use as the instructions for your income tax returns. Here again, the cruising sailor can bring some order out of the chaos by using a "dictionary" of lights. It is based on what the sailor sees, not on the type of vessel.

The twenty-two light situations shown in Figure D are ones which the cruising sailor is most likely to encounter. There are, of course, many other combinations and permutations of navigational light arrangements, but mastering these will free you from paging through a reference book during night sails in 90 percent of the cases.

This "dictionary" is based on the most distinctive lights. It does not always include all the running lights.

Finally, a few essential rules will clarify 90 percent of the situations you face in identifying navigational lights at night. First, whenever

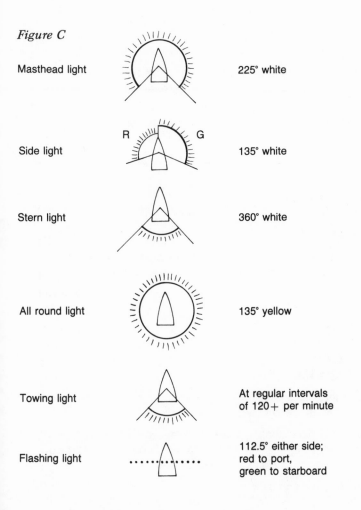

Figure C

Masthead light		225° white
Side light	R G	135° white
Stern light		360° white
All round light		135° yellow
Towing light		At regular intervals of 120+ per minute
Flashing light		112.5° either side; red to port, green to starboard

you see both side lights it can mean only one thing: you're on a collision course. Add to this a couple of white lights, one above the other, and what might have been a boat becomes a large ship. Get out of the way—fast.

Second, the two range lights on a large ship will, unless you're so close as to be under her bow, tell you her relative heading. The lower light will be positioned under the higher one.

Third, when your green starboard light faces a green light (or red to red) on another vessel, it's safe to proceed. You cannot be on a collision course. But, opposites attract. Beware of red facing green, or vice versa. You could be on a collision course.

179

Dictionary of Navigation Lights based on International Rules

SINGLE LIGHT

1. Green side light — Sailboat passing left to right. You have right of way.

2. Red side light — Sailboat passing right to left. You do not have right of way.

3. Combination red and green side light — Sailboat bow on

4. White all round light — Anchored vessel

5. White stern light — Stern of power or sail vessel. You are the overtaking vessel.

6. Yellow flashing light — Air cushion boat in non-displacement mode

VERTICAL ARRANGEMENT OF MORE THAN ONE LIGHT

7. One green light over one white light (both all round) — Trawler dragging nets

8. Two green lights (all round) — Usually seen with restricted maneuverability lights (No. 12 below). Dredger. Pass on this side.

9. One red over one green light (both all round) — Sailboat

10. One red light over one white (both all round) — Fishing boat, not trawling

11. Two red (all round) — Usually seen with restricted maneuverability lights (No. 12 below). Dredger. Do not pass on this side.

12. Two red and one white (all round) — Vessel with restricted maneuverability

13. Three red (all round) — Vessel constrained by draught

14. Two white (masthead) plus two red, one white (all round) — Vessel towing, restricted maneuverability

15. Two white (masthead)	Vessel towing, after end of tow less than 200 meters from bow
16. Two white masthead	Power vessel approaching
17. Three white masthead	Vessel towing, after end of tow more than 200 meters from bow
18. One white, one yellow (both stern lights)	Stern of towing vessel

NON-VERTICAL ARRANGEMENT

19. Two white all round lights	Large vessel at anchor
20. Two white masthead lights	Power vessel under way
21. Two white masthead lights, one red side light	Power vessel passing from right to left. You do not have right of way unless under sail.
22. Two white masthead lights, one green side light	Power vessel passing from left to right. You have right of way.

Leaking

Although the weather forecast was favorable, you encounter Force 6 and 7 winds after you round a cape on your three-day cruise. Your first landfall after the cape is a small island about 45 miles off the coast.

The wind is right on your nose, and your boat is taking solid water over the bows. Although you have reefed the main and hanked on a smaller headsail, the boat is still laboring under the strong sea conditions.

When one of your crew goes below to get sandwiches, he discovers water sloshing around above the cabin sole. He informs you of the situation, and you hurry below. It is obvious that a large leak is bringing in a great deal of water. The boat has only a plunger-style bilge pump.

What do you do?

HERE'S WHAT I'D DO . . .

Your first priority must be to put some of that water back where it came from. Detail one of your strongest crew members to start operating your old-fashioned Navy-style bilge pump.

But since even the most reliable pump (anything from a coffee can to a spiffy automatic electric rotary job) can only treat the symptom, you'd better start concentrating on discovering the cause of your leak.

You've been driving your boat fairly hard in those Force 6 winds and seas. Reduce sail and fall off the wind a bit to ease the strain. In wood boats, the leak may be caused by planks working in a seaway. This movement can easily make the seams part slightly, allowing water to enter. You may find that once you reduce the stress on the boat, the leaking will stop.

A far more common cause of leaking is defective through-hull fittings. Unfortunately, many newer boats are being constructed without seacocks. If a hose or any part of the related plumbing system should break, seawater pours into the hull, usually undiscovered until it appears above the cabin sole. The only solution in this case is to attempt to close the hose or pipe with waterproof tape, or bung the through-hull opening with a piece of wood. If seacocks are installed, as they should be, they can simply be closed.

It's possible that the seacocks need maintenance or renewing. Whenever you haul out, make the maintenance of your seacocks (not bottom cleaning!) your first priority. If you discover a seacock that needs new parts or replacement, it could take several days to complete repairs.

Another common cause of leaking in sailboats is siphoning. Once the continuous flow begins, usually when well heeled over, it can sink your boat. Assuming a through-hull fitting is under water at least part of the time (due to heeling over or design), and there is an open seacock, broken pipe or hose, or a stuck flapper valve, etc., the motion of your boat can start the siphoning phenomenon. Sea water will defy gravity and move up into the hull.

There are two solutions to this problem. Either close off the seacock, if fitted (preferably before getting under way), or loop the discharge hose or pipe and put a small vent in it at the top. Better yet, do both. The first makes it impossible for water to go in (or out). The second ensures that any reverse flow will stop when the pressure equalizes.

Some sailors, particularly those who use their auxiliary engine only under duress, forget or completely overlook one of the largest holes in their boat: that through which the propeller shaft passes. Here there is of course no seacock, since the opening can be neither opened or closed. The stuffing box prevents the sea from entering around the shaft. Adjusted properly, this fitting will allow a slow but steady drip to enter while the shaft is moving. Although rarely a site of massive leaking, the gland must be tightened whenever you secure your boat after motoring. Even the slowest drip will amount to gallons in a few days' time.

If you are singularly unfortunate and the leakage is caused by something as dramatic as a puncture in the hull, stopping the leak will require more heroic measures. You should make up a lead, copper, or plywood sheeting (gasketed with rags, cup grease, and whatever) to place over the hole. Shore these with mop handles, whisker poles, or any other piece of wood long enough to bridge the distance between the hole and a supporting vertical member.

A purpose-designed collision mat or one fashioned from settee cushions, blankets or spare sails, can be placed on the outside of the hull. Held by lines going clear around the boat, the water pressure will enhance its seal. If the hull puncture is near the water line, you may be able to heel the boat over to advantage by using moveable ballast.

Finally, if your boat is designed around the unitized construction concept, and entrance to the area of the leak is inhibited, don't be unwilling to dismantle the cabinetry and cabin sole with a fire axe or sledge hammer. This will be a small price to pay for effectively dealing with the leak.

Once you have discovered and cured the source of the leak, you can turn your full attention to getting the accumulated water out of your boat.

There are many types of bilge pumps. Some, like the coffee can, require fairly massive effort on the part of the operator, but are totally reliable. Others, the automatic electric ones being a good example, require little human effort but should not be relied on in an emergency. All, except the coffee can or bucket, are susceptible to clogging by the bits and pieces of junk which, like it or not, find their way into your boat's bilges. Strainers must be attached to the business end of your bilge pump plumbing to prevent this. When the chips are down, the last thing you want to be faced with is a perfectly good bilge pump that chokes to death on a cigarette wrapper.

Many cruising sailors are partial to the diaphragm-type hand-operated pump which can move a great deal of water in a short time. If you use one of this type, be sure that you carry extra parts in your spare parts box.

A bilge pump hose usually covers only a small area in the bilge and the water which you've accumulated must be able to get to it. The limber holes which are cut into the bottoms of the boat's floors and frames near the keel are designed to allow the accumulated water to drain to the hose intake. If they are clogged (which is usually the case), you won't be able to get all the water out with the finest pump in the world. The solution is to rig a small-gauge chain or piece of line through all the limber holes fore and aft: one line on the port side and one to starboard. A couple of tugs every once in a while should clear this passage.

Finally, if you have only one bilge pump, install a second. This is particularly important if your only pump is electrically operated. Even the most basic pump can self-destruct at the most inopportune moment. The long shaft is particularly vulnerable to being bent and rendered useless when an aggressive pumper bashes against it as the boat heels over. When all else fails, a bucket is efficient, completely reliable, and maintenance-free. Be sure you have at least one aboard.

SITUATION 42:
The Sailings

You are preparing for a passage from Key West, Florida, to Pensacola. While checking and updating your charts for this trip, you discover that you have no small scale chart which includes both Key West and Pensacola, although you have plenty of large scale charts for the entire journey.

Without an inclusive chart, you cannot plot your course or measure its distance graphically. The proper chart is not available at the local chandlery, nor can you borrow it.

How can you determine course and distance to Pensacola?

HERE'S WHAT I'D DO . . .

SITUATION 42 Recommended Solution

Although rarely used these days due to the wide availability of small scale charts, there are several techniques you can use to determine course and distance without having the chart. As a group, these techniques are called "The Sailings."

The trigonometry required scares most people away immediately, but it is so straightforward that even the least mathematically minded cruising sailor can handle it without losing his temper. An investment in an electronic calculator reduces the calculations to simple button-pushing.

Most of "The Sailings" simply assume away the fact that the earth is spherical. They treat it as a plane, thus gaining simplicity but giving up somewhat in accuracy. One "sailing," however, known as "Middle Latitude," compensates for most of the errors due to treating the earth as if it were flat. It also has the advantage of being very easy to work with. Consequently, you'll use it to plan your trip to the mainland.

Before you begin, however, you'll have to know just two things: the position of Key West, Florida, and the position of Pensacola. This information is easy enough to get. Latitude and longitude will be shown on each of the separate charts. If, in an extreme case, you do not have charts, you can look up the positions in a "Maritime Position Index," similar to the one in Appendix S in *Bowditch,* a book which every cruising sailor should have on board.

After a bit of research with your two charts, you find that Key West, Florida is in latitude 24°33′ North, longitude 81°49′ West; Pensacola is in latitude 30°24′ North, longitude 87°13′ West.

Once you have both positions, there is nothing left but some very simple arithmetic. Three formulas guide you to a course and distance.

The first calculates a value called "departure." This is simply a translation of the *angular difference* in longitude between Key West and Pensacola into *nautical miles.* The formula compensates for the fact that lines of longitude converge at higher latitudes. Although the angle may remain the same, the number of nautical miles "in" the angle gets smaller.

For example, at the equator, 60 degrees of longitude is, as you would expect, equal to 3600 nautical miles; one degree equals 60 nautical miles. But, at latitude 30 degrees (North or South), the linear distance is only 3118 miles. For this reason, the formula uses an average latitude, called "mid-latitude," to scale the linear distance down.

The formula for "departure" is:

departure = difference in longitude (in minutes) × cosine of mid-latitude

In this case, the difference in longitude in minutes is:

$$\begin{array}{r} 87°13' \text{ West} \\ -81°49' \text{ West} \\ \hline 5°24' \text{ or 324 minutes} \end{array}$$

To determine mid-latitude, first determine the difference in latitude between your present location and your destination:

$$\begin{array}{r} 30°24' \text{ North} \\ -24°33' \text{ North} \\ \hline 5°51' \end{array}$$

Then divide by two to get an average:

$$5°51' \div 2 = 2°55.5'$$

Now add the average to your present latitude:

$$\begin{array}{r} 24°33' \\ + 2°55.5' \\ \hline 27°28.5' \end{array}$$

Since the cosine of 27°28.5' is .88722 (calculated using a slide rule, pocket calculator or logarithmic table), departure is then equal to:

$$324 \times .8872 = 287.45$$

From here on, it is a matter of solving a right triangle, using very basic trigonometry. In this case, the triangle looks like Figure A. The difference in latitude between Key West and Pensacola is 5°51'. Since minutes of latitude, unlike those of longitude, do not vary in linear distance as latitude changes, the corresponding number of nautical

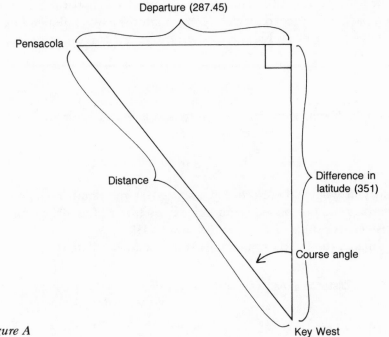

Departure (287.45)

Pensacola

Distance

Difference in
latitude (351)

Course angle

Figure A   Key West

miles can be calculated directly: 5°51′ = 351 nautical miles.

With two sides of known length, you can calculate the Course Angle, using the second of the three formulae:

Tangent of the *Departure*
Course Angle = Difference in latitude
     in minutes

     = 287.45/351

     = .819

Course Angle = 39°19′

Although this is the course angle, it may not be the course to steer to get to Pensacola. Take another look at the relative positions of Key West and Pensacola. Then, label the course angle accordingly. In this case, common sense interpretations of the two positions tells you that your destination (Pensacola) is northwest of Key West. The course angle is, therefore, labelled as follows:

N 39°19′ *W*

191

Since the prefix in the label is "N," start at the north point on the compass and proceed clockwise or counterclockwise, depending on whether the suffix is East or West. In this case it is West, so the course to Pensacola is

$$360° - 39°19' = 320°41'$$

If you had been proceeding *from* Pensacola *to* Key West, the labelling of the course angle would have been:

$$S\ 39°19'\ E$$

and you would, therefore, have started at the South point on the compass and proceeded counterclockwise toward East. The course in this case would be $180° - 39°19' = 140°41'$.

Finally, the third formula tells you how to calculate distance.

Distance in nautical miles   =   *difference in latitude in miles*
                                                 cosine of course angle

    =   351/cosine 39°19'

    =   351/.77366

    =   453.4 nautical miles

Although using The Sailings is an easy way to calculate course and distance when the right chart is not available, proceed with extreme care. They provide no warning of navigational hazards. For this you need the proper charts.

SITUATION 43:
Salvage

While cruising Lake Superior, you decide to put into one of the Apostle Islands to take on provisions.

As you head down the channel separating the island from the mainland, the weather begins to deteriorate. When the small harbor entrance comes into view, you have reefed down for the Force 6 winds. A nasty chop is coming right at you out of the south.

When you reach the harbor entrance, you attempt to start your engine, but are unsuccessful. Since the wind is coming directly out of the small channel, beating your way in is out of the question.

A power boat appears at the outer end of the breakwater and heads toward you, the skipper waving. He comes alongside and shouts that he saw you were in trouble, and offers to tow you into the harbor. As he comes closer, one of his crew leaps aboard with tow line in hand. Once he has secured it he offers to steer, saying that he "knows the way in."

The next day, as you are preparing to get under way, you are presented with a $2,000 salvage claim.

What should you have done to avoid this situation?

HERE'S WHAT I'D DO . . .

SITUATION 43 Recommended Solution

Usually other boaters who offer to give a hand when you are in trouble want nothing more than a friendly thank you for their efforts. But, from a legal point of view, they have every right to charge you for their aid. These charges may seem excessive once the excitement has died down.

"Salvage" is defined as "the act of saving a vessel from great danger such as perils of the sea." Although you may feel that the danger you faced off the harbor entrance was minor, an admiralty court might disagree. For example, successful salvage claims have been made for towing done in calm waters when a boat has run out of fuel.

You can contest the claim in court, of course. But if it sticks, it is your boat that owes the money, not you. This means that a lien could be placed against your boat. It could be sold at auction if you did not pay the $2,000.

Although sea law is very complicated, there are some basic things you could have done to minimize the chance of a successful salvage claim.

Certainly, you should not have allowed the crew member of the power boat to come aboard. Although he came aboard to provide "help" in rigging the line, his presence only strengthens the claim for payment.

Also, you should have used *your* line for a tow line, not his. And allowing the stranger to steer was, in effect, turning command of the operation over to the skipper of the power boat. If you are going to accept a tow, be certain that *you* remain in control of the overall undertaking.

An agreement should have been reached before the tow began. This should deal with what charges, if any, are to be levied. Although it is usually difficult to make this agreement in writing, your presence and that of any others should be noted in the log as witnesses to a verbal bargain.

As soon as possible after the agreement was made, you should have entered all the relevant details of the incident in the logbook, since "degree of danger" will be carefully evaluated using this, and other, evidence.

Ninety-nine percent of the time, the Good Samaritan who happens by at the right time is just that, a sailor who believes in the ancient tradition of helping others in distress. But, next time you run aground while poking around a river or bay, consider kedging your way off instead of accepting a quick pull from a passer-by. It could save you a lot of money.

SITUATION 44:

Determining Deviation

You've just completed a 65-mile crossing during which you sailed in company with another boat about the same size as your 30-foot sloop.

To your surprise, however, your friends in the other boat drew further and further away from their position abeam of you. By early afternoon, they were barely in sight almost five miles north of your position.

When your landfall finally came into sight, you understood why they set a more northerly course. You were a good ten miles south of the position you were heading for.

You are certain that you factored variation into your course calculation properly. Consequently, you must review your table of compass deviation.

How do you ascertain your compass deviation?

HERE'S WHAT I'D DO . . .

SITUATION 44 Recommended Solution

Every cruising sailor should know how to determine compass error —the difference between true bearing or direction and compass bearing or direction.

Compass error consists of two components: variation and deviation. The first, a function of variability in the earth's magnetic field, is given on sailing charts and can be treated as a "known." The second is a function of the magnetism of your boat. It is never the same for any two boats in the same area and it changes with the boat's heading. It can be treated as a "known" only after you (or a compass adjustor) have calculated it for your boat.

There are many different ways to figure out your compass's deviation. Each, however, requires an understanding of two fundamental rules.

The first rule helps you to know if the deviation you've discovered is easterly or westerly. Deviation must always be labelled one or the other, or it would be impossible to apply the necessary correction to your compass reading. The first rule is as follows:

> Whenever the *compass* bearing is greater than the *magnetic* bearing (true bearing corrected for variation), deviation is west; if the compass bearing is less than the magnetic bearing, deviation is east.

The first rule is easy to remember if you use the mnemonic "Compass least, error east; compass best, error west."

The second fundamental rule enables you to apply the deviation a discovered in order to translate true or magnetic courses or bearings into compass courses or bearings. This rules states that:

> Whenever you convert directions from true to magnetic or compass, you *add* westerly deviation and sub-

tract easterly deviation. Conversely, if you are converting from compass direction to magnetic or true, you *subtract* westerly deviation and add easterly deviation.

Any confusion arising from the second rule can be minimized by committing the following to memory:

	True
Add	Variation
West	Magnetic
	Deviation
	Compass

Sailors of the last century, known more for their daring than their intellect, relied on creative memory devices to deal with this rule, among them: "True Virgins Make Dead Company" and (with the order reversed), "Can Dead Men Vote Twice?"

An example will demonstrate both rules at work.

Let's say you have located a range of two lighthouses a few miles away on the shore line. They are both shown clearly on your chart. The true direction of the range is 035 degrees. The chart also tells you that variation in the area is 10° West. Your compass, as you sight across its vanes onto the range, shows a bearing of 049 degrees.

Since deviation is the difference between magnetic and compass course, bearing or heading, you must first determine the magnetic bearing of the range. Use the second rule to make this conversion.

	True Bearing	035°
Add	Variation	010° W
West	Magnetic	045°
	Deviation	—
	Compass	—

You know there is some deviation, since there is a difference between the magnetic bearing and your compass bearing. But, it must be given magnitude (in degrees) and direction (East or West). This is most easily done by using the first rule (Compass least, error east; compass best, error west).

```
              True       035°
          Variation      010°W
   Add    Magnetic       045°
  West    Deviation      4°W
          Compass        049°
```

Combining both rules provides a good cross-check, as in the above example.

It would be great if that was all there was to it. You'd simply apply the 4° W correction each time you converted the magnetic course or bearing to the compass course or bearing. But, as stated earlier, deviation varies with the heading of your boat. Consequently, you'll have to compare your compass reading with magnetic bearings on more than one heading. In fact, most cruising sailors recommend that you do it for at least every ten or 15 degrees around the compass.

How do you accomplish this?

One of the easiest ways is to compare your compass with another of known reliability. Place this compass somewhere on your boat where it will be unaffected by any ferrous metal. Mount it temporarily high above the deck. Be sure that it is aligned properly with the other compass's lubber's line. Then, swing the boat around using the dinghy or warps, steadying up and comparing readings as you go 'round. For each position, deviation is the difference between the two compasses. You can apply the first rule to determine direction.

"Run in a range" is another way to check for deviation. During cruises, you are bound to see range lights or daymarkers plotted on your charts or mentioned in your pilot books. Never pass up an opportunity to compare the reading of your compass with the magnetic bearing of the range taken off the chart. Once again, any difference between the magnetic bearing and your compass's reading is deviation.

A similar approach is to determine deviation by running several visible courses. This can best be done from one navigational aid to another, such as marked channel buoys. Although the course between the marks may not be shown on the chart, you can easily determine it. Any difference between the plotted magnetic course and your boat's heading is deviation. Determine direction by applying the first rule.

"Swinging ship" is a classic way to determine how much deviation your compass has. You can run across a range (or do it at anchor, using your dinghy to pull the bow or stern around) on different headings ten or fifteen degrees apart. When you compare the magnetic bearing of the range with the compass bearings on each heading, you can calculate deviation. This approach can also be used on a distant object—at least six miles distant—assuming your position is known with accuracy. Once you've finished, you can check the accuracy of your work by calculating the average of the compass bearings. It should coincide with the magnetic direction. This is based on the fact that total westerly deviation should be about equal to total easterly deviation as you take bearings at equidistant points around the compass.

Celestial bodies can also be used to help you determine deviation. Except for the moon, their true bearing is almost the same for rising as setting, one being to the east and one to the west. True north or south is midway between the two values. The difference between this value and 180 (or 000 as the case may be) is compass error. Once you've removed the effect of variation, you can calculate deviation. For example, assume that you take a bearing on the sun when it rises in the morning and when it sets that evening. Your morning bearing is 084 degrees and your evening is 280 degrees. The midpoint between the two values is 182 degrees (084 + 280 ÷ 2). The difference between 182° and 180° is 2°. This is compass error. From your chart, you determine that variation in the area is 5° W. Using the second rule, you can calculate deviation:

	True	180°
Add	Variation	5°W
West	Magnetic	185°
	Deviation	3°E
	Compass	182°

Another approach is to run reciprocal courses. Starting at any fixed point such as a navigational buoy, steer steadily away on an easily held course. After you have gone a half-mile or more (but can still see the buoy), drop a disposable buoy over the side. Quickly execute a button-hook turn and steady up on the range made up of the disposable buoy and the original mark. Run straight down this range to the original mark without reference to the compass. When you are steadied up on

202

the return course, read the compass. If the reading is not the recipro-cal of your outbound course, deviation is present.

It's reasonable to assume that the deviation on the reciprocal course is equal and opposite; hence you can calculate it easily. For example, if your outbound course (by compass) was 270° and your inbound compass course was 080 degrees, deviation is present. Its magnitude is one-half the difference between 260 degrees (the reciprocal of your inbound course) and 270 degrees, or 5 degrees. But you do not yet know its direction. This requires knowledge of the magnetic course, for which there is an easy formula. Magnetic course is midway be-tween the inbound course and the reciprocal of the outbound course. Thus, magnetic course in this case is 080° + 090° ÷ 2 = 085°. Using either rule, you can now give the deviation direction: it is easterly.

When you're in the northern hemisphere, Polaris, the polestar, can be used to check for deviation. It's never more than two degrees away from true north for observers anywhere between the equator and 60° North. For greater accuracy, you can use the tables in nautical al-manacs, which give corrected azimuths, although for a reasonably accurate quick check of compass deviation, this should not be needed.

Finally, you can use "amplitudes" (bearings of the sun when it is rising and setting) to determine deviation. This method requires that you know your approximate latitude (this should be no problem), and the declination of the sun (which can be found in an almanac). Tables 27 and 28 in *Bowditch* can then be used to calculate amplitude. All you need to do is to compare the true amplitude with your compass bearing. This yields compass error, from which you can remove varia-tion to get deviation. For example, assume the area's variation to be 24° E. If the true amplitude is calculated to be 110° and the observed compass bearing of the sun when rising was 088°, deviation can be calculated using the second rule.

	True	110°
Add	Variation	24°E
West	Magnetic	086°
	Deviation	2° W
	Compass	088°

To counter the effects of refraction, take your bearing when the sun's lower limb is about one-half diameter above the horizon.

Navigating Around Headlands

You are single-handing your 28-foot sloop on a 160-mile cruise up the coast. The route is straightforward coastwise sailing with plenty of landmarks and lights to pilot by.

Around 11 P.M. on your first night out, a gale kicks up when you are just south of a major headland. Even in the strong winds and seas, you manage to hold your course of 010° True.

Your last fix, plotted just ten minutes ago, puts you seven miles due south of the lighthouse which stands at the outer edge of the promontory.

You know that there are dangerous rocks located three miles due west of the lighthouse. Unfortunately, according to the latest *Notices to Mariners,* the light buoy marking this danger is not operating.

In better conditions, you might hug the coast and take the narrow channel between the headland and the shoal, but certainly not tonight.

You dash below to get the chart in order to plot your course around the danger. As you return to the cockpit, a particularly strong gust rips it out of your hand. It disappears into the night.

Without the chart, how can you clear the off-lying danger?

HERE'S WHAT I'D DO . . .

SITUATION 45 Recommended Solution

First, your recent fix placed you seven miles from the lighthouse at the edge of the headland. If you turned immediately to port and placed the lighthouse on your beam, and then kept it there by small course adjustments, you'd maintain your seven mile distance. You'd clear the rocks by four miles, as shown in Figure A.

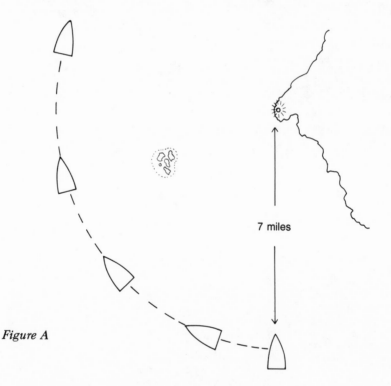

7 miles

Figure A

When you use this technique, be sure that you keep the lighthouse near, but never forward of, your beam.

Since this is far from an exact approach, you'll want to make estimates of your distance from the lighthouse (and thereby the rocks) as frequently as possible as you round the headland. If you have a distance log aboard, it's simple.

Just observe the rate at which the heading of your boat changes while you keep the lighthouse abeam. During a change of 57.5 degrees, the distance off is about the same as the distance your boat has travelled. For a 28.5 degrees change, the distance is about equal to twice the boat's run. For 19 degrees, it's about three times the run, and for 14.5 degrees, it's four times the run.

Another approach is to use the so-called Rule of Sixty. It will tell you how much to alter course to clear the rocks by any distance you select. Although the calculations may not immediately make sense to you, they'll enable you to steer a safe course without making continuous course changes. You won't be faced with the problem of keeping the lighthouse on your beam.

Here's how it works: Divide 60 (a constant value no matter what the situation) by 7 (your current distance from the lighthouse). The result is approximately 8.6. Now, determine how close to the lighthouse you wish to pass. Let's assume it to be seven miles, as in the previous example.

Multiply 7 by 8.6. The result is 60.2. This is the course adjustment you must make to clear the lighthouse by seven miles. Your new course will be 309.8 degrees.

Although you may find both of these techniques helpful in a pinch, they'll only provide you with estimates. Use them with caution and never in place of proper charts.

NOTES

NOTES

NOTES

NOTES

NOTES